7

Thanks to the American Soldier, whose
sacrifices for freedom make this book possible.

LDR Investments LLP
To purchase this Guide, visit our Web site at www.LDRinvest.com

info@LDRinvest.com

First Edition, July 2012

ISBN: 978-0-9854061-0-3

Editor: Mary Brandt Kerr, Ergo Editorial Services, Inc.
Design: Bruce Sanders Design and Illustration, Inc.
Printed by Lightning Source, Inc., La Vergne, TN

Printed in the United States of America

I believe it is my duty to make money and to use the money I make for the good of my fellow man.

—John D. Rockefeller
Industrialist

Introduction

Despite having vastly different Army experiences with deployments to different theaters of war, each of us came to share a concern that our combat-focused Army is struggling to financially educate Soldiers. As junior officers we have frequently seen Soldiers struggling with the results of bad financial decisions. And financial education—if it was available at all—was offered after problems developed. As Army leaders one of our primary responsibilities is to be proactive in keeping Soldiers safe—including financially safe—so we set out to provide a guide that would be useful for this purpose.

After leading our individual platoons through one-on-one financial counseling, question and answer briefings and company internal review sessions, we identified that our concern was widespread and there was a real need for an easy-to-read reference guide to Army-related financial questions.

Our intent is that this Guide, by providing an easily accessible resource of information, will help prevent some of the financial difficulties Soldiers sometimes find themselves in. We hope that this book will be used by future platoon leaders, platoon sergeants and company commanders throughout the Army.

While we recognize that this is only a first step, it will be a foundation to providing an upgrade for the level of financial education available. This book can be used by leaders and subordinates alike, referenced by Soldiers and their families, used in barracks rooms, homes, briefing tents and headquarters buildings; our goal is to help improve the financial future of our Soldiers.

Our duty remains to help protect our country and do everything in our power to take care of Soldiers. If this Guide succeeds in increasing the level of financial awareness and responsibility of our Soldiers, then it will be playing an important role in accomplishing both.

—Lauren Gore, Rich Sexton, J.D. Dolan
Washington, DC, July, 2012

Contents

My favorite things in life don't cost any money. It's really clear that the most precious resource we all have is time.

—Steve Jobs
American Entrepreneur

Savings

Bottom Line Up Front (BLUF):
Saving and budgeting techniques and the power of compound interest —all of which will help you avoid or get out of the 'rat race'.
- Pay yourself first
- Savings techniques
- Budgeting
- Power of compound interest

Discussion:
Pay yourself first means—every time you receive a paycheck, you save a certain pre-determined percentage of your income. You can automatically deduct this amount from your paycheck through Defense Finance & Accounting Services (DFAS), your unit's finance representative or you can set up an automatic savings plan through your bank.

Spend Less and Save More!
The majority of Soldiers and civilians alike can spend less money and save more. Many people think that they are financially "stretched to the limit," when in reality, they earn enough to save but continue to spend more than is necessary. The ability to make the difficult decisions—the harder right, not the easier wrong —is what will set us apart and enable us to save more, earlier. Spending will always be one of the greatest financial challenges that everyone faces: those of us who learn to spend effectively and within our means will gain financial independence, while those of us who cannot master the ability to keep our spending under control will struggle and continue to live "paycheck to paycheck." Learn to save more and spend less and your salary as a Soldier will help set you free from the "rat race" that so many Americans endure.

Saving Techniques
Many of us spend money that we could be saving. To stretch your paycheck, refer to the Top 10 Ways to Cut Spending (see next page) and modify your spending habits: the goal of saving money is to put more cash into your pocket at the end of each month. A greater amount of discretionary cash

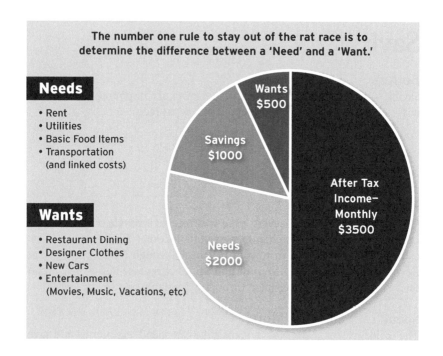

The number one rule to stay out of the rat race is to determine the difference between a 'Need' and a 'Want.'

Needs
- Rent
- Utilities
- Basic Food Items
- Transportation (and linked costs)

Wants
- Restaurant Dining
- Designer Clothes
- New Cars
- Entertainment (Movies, Music, Vacations, etc)

Wants $500

Savings $1000

Needs $2000

After Tax Income— Monthly $3500

usually means that you will use less credit card debt to pay for the things that you really need or truly want.

Top 10 Ways to Cut Spending

1) **Big purchases.** Distinguish between what is a 'want' (i.e. Mustang GT) and what is a 'need' (i.e. Ford Focus).
2) **Shop around.** Use online merchants like Amazon or eBay to price compare and as benchmark-pricing tools.
3) **Delayed spending.** So you want a 52-inch TV? Do the research and find the brand/make/model that you want and set a goal for one year from today to buy that model. This will enable you to put your budget into motion and save for something that will cost significantly less in one year.
4) **Meal planning.** Plan out your meals by preparing them for the workday. Your diet will be healthier—better than your battle buddy's fast food— and cheaper.

5) **Energy savers.** Use programmable thermostats which turn off/ down when you aren't in the house and turn on/up when you come home. These pay for themselves and save money each month on your utility bill. You may also qualify for certain tax incentives. (**www.eere.energy.gov**)

6) **Pre-owned.** Products you can find that are in "like new" condition with up to 30% off.

7) **Frozen credit card.** Literally put your credit card in a bowl of water and freeze it. This will eliminate any impulse buying, but will allow you the flexibility of having the credit card for emergencies.

8) **Carpool.** Saves on gas, tolls, and you share the burden of wear-and-tear on your vehicle.

9) **Generic over-the-counter medicines.** Almost identical ingredients and 30% less expensive. Also don't forget about the on-post hospital for routine medicines like headache pills.

10) **Drink tap water.** Tap water in the U.S. is as clean if not cleaner than bottled water. If you do not like the taste of tap water, buy a coal filter for your faucet.

Budgeting

A budget allows you to do two things: (1) gain visibility of your spending down to the dollar, and (2) provide a blueprint for your monthly expenses. With a well-formed budget, you already have the answers to the test, and the starting point for what it will take for you to achieve financial freedom.

Forming a Budget

- Track your spending. The website **www.mint.com** is highly recommended as a modern and technological approach to personal budgeting. Regardless of the method you choose, the important action is setting a budget. You can try the 'old-fashioned' pen and paper budgeting method, but you may find it tedious, time consuming, and human error is common—these common setbacks that are the primary reasons budgeting fails. But remember: the systems are already available, you just need to put them in place and use them consistently.
- Distinguish between a **need** and a **want.**
- Focus on the basics: house, car, insurance, food, daycare, etc.

- Limit anything that does not fall into the need category.
- The 15% of Income Rule: Regardless of your income, you should aim to save at least 15% of each paycheck.
- Automatic savings is the best policy. Set up automatic deductions that will draw a percentage of your paycheck and place it into an account of your choice: TSP, Roth IRA, Traditional Deductible IRA, savings account, etc. This will 'force' you to save and prepare for the future.
- Be realistic. Do not set yourself up for failure. Your budget needs to be reasonable and, more importantly, sustainable. Give yourself the standard 5-10% buffer during your initial planning considerations.

Apply the Squeeze

You used to "eat out" every day for both breakfast and lunch; after reading this book you decide that it is much cheaper and healthier to fix your breakfast and lunch every day.

Thus, you save $5 on every meal. You do some quick math and realize that you are **saving $70** (two meals a day at $5 each, seven days a week). Every Sunday you put $70 into a jar. At the end of the month you deposit $280 into your savings account. You never felt the pinch because you made a lifestyle change and took advantage of the 'squeeze' technique by **saving over $3,640 in a year.**

Sticking to Your Budget

Before any purchase ask yourself these questions:

a. Does this make me more efficient at my job or my family more secure?

b. Can I get the same thing cheaper somewhere else (think vending machines)?

c. How long will this last and how often will I use it?

d. How is this particular item trending? Can I get it for half the price if I wait six months?

"Bonus" pay comes throughout the year in the form of income tax refunds, reenlistment bonuses, gifts, etc, and can be a huge help to your budget. Save at least 40% of any unexpected money and plan to automatically save 40% of any expected pay raises, through DFAS or automatic saving, preferably

The most difficult aspect of all this is having the self-discipline to avoid the temptation of small daily consumption purchases.

BEFORE the pay increase hits your paycheck and you get used to having the extra money to spend.

The **squeeze** is a savings technique that helps you break your old spending habits without feeling the pain. Squeezing does not hurt, however most people avoid 'squeezing' their saving and choose instead to wait until they want something and realize they do not have the $3,000 or whatever it costs, and immediately turn to their credit cards. The squeeze is the safer and cheaper alternative to purchasing on credit, and it requires putting a little money away every day, whether it is $1 or $20, so that at the end of the week, month or year you have accumulated enough savings to purchase those planned or unexpected items. The best way to squeeze is to closely monitor your spending, identify wasteful spending habits, items and services that you can live without, and put whatever money you would normally spend on these expenses towards savings.

So what is the hardest part? The most difficult aspect of all this is having the self-discipline to avoid the temptation of small daily consumption purchases. Plan and prepare your food each day, avoid buying the energy drinks at the gas station (get more sleep), etc. Now take a look at what that money can do for you if you are successful in cutting the fat out of your spending and sticking to a budget. **With money saved from avoiding the vending machine, you can take your significant other out for a nice steak dinner or reward your kids with a trip to the amusement park—all without using a credit card!**

Savings Deposit Program (SDP) is one of the best deals out there for eligible, deployed Soldiers. The SDP was established to provide a place to deposit money for savings purposes to service members who serve in designated combat zones. Some of the benefits and guidelines are:
• Eligibility—Deployed to combat zones, qualified hazardous duty areas, or certain contingency operations outside of the United States for more than 30 days.

Each Soldier should strive to save from three to six months' living expenses.

- Interest—the SDP provides Soldiers the opportunity to deposit money into a savings account at an annual rate of 10% which compounds quarterly. Your federal income is tax-free while deployed in a hazardous duty zone, but the interest accrued on earnings deposited into the SDP is taxable.
- Deposits—Eligible Soldiers may deposit all or part of their non-allotted pay into a Department of Defense savings account. Up to $10,000 may be deposited in this account during a single deployment.
- Non-allotted pay is the amount of money a Soldier is entitled to receive, less authorized deductions.
- Deposits cannot be less than $5, must be in multiples of $5 and cannot exceed a service member's monthly non-allotted current pay and allowances (e.g. monthly net pay after all deductions and allotments; includes special pay and reenlistment bonus).
- Soldiers are asked to contact their finance office to open the account and to make deposits. The last day to make a deposit into the fund is the date of departure from the assignment. However, interest will accrue for up to 90 days after return from deployment.
- If your account contains over $10,000 due to interest you can make quarterly requests to withdraw the balance that exceeds $10,000. The $10,000 remains in the account until the service member's eligibility terminates and the remaining funds are entirely withdrawn. *Note: Withdrawing the $10,000 before leaving the combat zone is not authorized, unless there is an emergency. For more information reference:* **www.dfas.mil/dfas/militarymembers/payentitlements/sdp.html.**

The Time Value of Money—Save Early, Save Often

"Rule of 72"
Use this rule to calculate how many years it will take to double your money at a specified interest rate. For example, $1,000 earning 6% per year will double in 12 years (divide 72 by the given interest rate (six) and it will give the years estimated for your initial investment to double = 12).

The initial small amounts that you are saving create large returns in the long-run. Although 10% is an ambitious return, the most important takeaway is how hard your money works when you contribute early. $10 to $20 a day can be easily saved once you establish your budget and put into practice some of the saving techniques already discussed. Look at a daily contribution and you will be amazed at how small daily savings result in major returns.

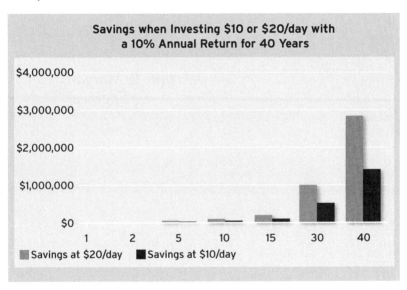

Emergency Funds
Each Soldier should strive to save from three to six months' of living expenses. Your money should be kept in an easily accessible savings or money market account, not in a long-term investment asset (refer to the Investments chapter for details). Only use this 'pot' of money for an emergency.

Final Note

The foundation for your financial freedom starts today by establishing a budget and beginning a savings and investment plan; you should not wait to invest in your future. This is *your* future!

Preparation for old age should begin not later than one's teens.

—Arthur E. Morgan
Engineer

Retirement

BLUF:
Saving for retirement needs to start as soon as possible. This chapter will provide a synopsis of the three main types of retirement vehicles: Roth IRA, Traditional Deductible IRA and the Thrift Savings Plan (TSP).

Discussion:
Planning for retirement is the easiest way to secure your financial future, but it is imperative to start immediately in order to maximize compound interest on those savings. Of the three methods, there is no wrong choice: the only way to fail is to not invest for retirement at all. A good benchmark is to set a goal of saving between 10 and 20 percent of your annual income. And remember: in order to maximize your returns and reduce your risk you must start investing as early as possible to allow compound interest to work for you.

Retirement Options
In the military you have three primary financial vehicles to be used for retirement. Think of each of these three vehicles as a "shopping bag"—not investments, but each can **hold** investments for you. The chapter on Investments will discuss specific investment opportunities, while the specific retirement vehicles are explained on the next page.

Roth IRA

SGT Jones, age 30, made a Roth IRA contribution of $2,000 in 2005. In 2012 SGT Jones' Roth IRA has a balance of $3,500. SGT Jones decides to close his Roth IRA in a non-qualified distribution. Since the distribution is non-qualified, SGT Jones will owe taxes on his Roth earnings of $1,500, and will pay tax on this amount at his marginal tax rate. In addition, since SGT Jones has not reached age $59\frac{1}{2}$, and since he did not meet any of the exceptions, he will also be assessed an early withdrawal penalty on the earnings. If we assume that SGT Jones is in the 28% marginal tax bracket, he will pay $420 in tax on the earnings, and will pay a 10% penalty in the amount of $150 on the early distribution.

	Roth IRA	Traditional Deductible IRA	Thrifts Savings Plan (TSP)
PROS	• Money isn't taxed when you take it out • Your own money can be withdrawn without penalty • Lots of variety in providers	• Money contributed is tax–deferred • Lots of variety in providers	• Easy set up; comes straight out of pre–tax dollars. • Deductions are shown on every LES • Penalty–free loan
CONS	• Earnings can't be withdrawn without penalty until owner is 59 $1/2$	• Your money is taxed when you withdraw • Money can't be withdrawn without penalty until owner is 59 $1/2$	• Limited online management capabilities • Money is taxed upon withdrawal
OVERALL	• $5k max annual contribution	• Useful as an alternative to the TSP • $5k max annual contribution	• Taxed the same as a Traditional IRA • $17k max annual contribution

Individual Retirement Accounts

Two of the most common forms of IRAs are the Roth and the Traditional Deductible. The major difference between these two forms is deductibility. Deductible income allows you to lower your taxable income and therefore get taxed on less money. The extent of the benefits associated with lowering taxable income is discussed in the Taxes chapter. Both are retirement financial vehicles for individuals. As a Soldier you can max out your TSP and your Roth IRA in the same year. With a TSP annual contribution limit of $17,000 and a Roth maximum contribution limit of $5,000, many Soldiers will not be able to invest to the full amount; however, most Soldiers will be able to contribute something from each paycheck. As with most big things in life, including financial security for you and your family, it begins with taking the first small step.

For further education on the tax implications of these investments, read the regulations laid out in Publication 590 at **www.irs.gov**.

Roth IRA

A Roth IRA **is taxed when you put money into it.** The largest advantage is seen when you withdraw the money from a **Roth IRA: none of it—and that includes the earnings derived from compound interest— will be taxed,** assuming that the Roth IRA has been open for at least five tax years and you are older than age 59 ½ (there are steep penalties for withdrawing the earnings early). The growth of your money is going to come from compounding.

Traditional Deductible IRA

The Traditional Deductible IRA is tax-deferred. You can put money into this account before taxes are taken out. The kicker is that when you withdraw money from this account **you will be taxed for those withdrawals.** For more details on the IRA, check out the sites below:

www.beginnersinvest.about.com
www.tsp.gov/planningtools
www.irs.gov (publication 590 is all about IRAs)

Early Withdrawal Penalty Exceptions	
Disability	• Don't consider until you review IRS Code for disability definition
Medical	• Unreimbursed medical expenses • Must exceed 7.5% of adjusted gross income • Medical insurance premiums after IRA owner has received unemployment compensation for more than 12 weeks • Death of owner
Home Purchase	• Must be first home • Up to $10,000 penalty and tax-free, if the money has been in the account for five years
Education	• IRA owner and family members • Reference IRA article 97-60 • You may still owe federal income tax
Taxes	• Pay back taxes because of an IRS levy placed against IRA

Thrift Savings Plan (TSP)

The Federal Thrift Savings Plan (TSP) is a retirement savings and investment plan for federal employees. A TSP is incredibly easy to set up and is tracked directly on your LES. The money allocated to your TSP (on a percentage basis) is taken out of your paycheck and invested before being taxed.

Tax Deferred (TSP & Traditional Deductible IRA)

By paying less income tax, you have more take-home pay than if you had saved an equal amount that was not excluded from taxable income.

For example, you are saving through a before-tax contributions vehicle, such as the TSP or Traditional Deductible IRA. You earn $30,000 taxable income per year, which places you in the 15% tax bracket. If you contribute 5% each month (or $1,500 per year) to your TSP/IRA account, you will likely **save $225** in federal taxes (15% (your tax bracket) x $1,500 = $225). If you had simply deposited the $1,500 in a savings account, you would have owed $225 in federal taxes. Your tax savings will be even greater if the state in which you live (or of which you are considered a legal resident) allows you to exclude TSP contributions from taxable income, as most states do. The money in your IRA will grow in a tax-deferred manner until you start to withdraw your funds after age 59 $1/2$.

It is important to note, however, that every dollar you withdraw will be 100% taxable at the time of withdrawal. Reference **www.TSP.gov** for the most updated information.

Whereas with the Roth IRA and the Traditional Deductible IRA there are an unlimited number of investments to put in them, with the TSP, there are just six primary investment choices. Please refer to the TSP Investment Options graph to get a feel for the investment options and the amount of risk you will be exposing yourself to in five of the six choices. (With the sixth choice, the "L"—Lifetime Fund—there are a number of target dates from which you can pick. Each one starts with a different level of risk.)

	Key rule: More Risk = Possibility of Larger Return	
Risk	**TSP Investment Options**	
Low	G Fund	**Government Securities Investment Fund** Invested in short-term, low-fee U.S. Treasury Securities that are specially issued to the TSP.
Medium Low	F Fund	**Fixed Income Index** Investment Fund–invested in a bond index fund that tracks the Barclay Capital's U.S. Aggregate bond index.
Medium	C Fund	**Common Stock Index Fund** Invested in a stock index fund that tracks large companies included in the Standard & Poor's (S&P) 500 stock index.
Medium High	S Fund	**Small Capitalization Stock Index Investment Fund** Invested in a stock index fund that tracks medium and small companies included in the Wilshire 4500 stock index.
High	I Fund	**International Stock Index Investment Fund** Invested in a stock index fund that tracks 21 different companies included in the European and the Far Eastern Stock Index.

Military Retirement

The military retirement program is arguably one of the best pensions in the world. With 20 years of service (which is the basis of our figures), you receive 50% of your base pay upon retirement. All charts and figures use the 2012 military pay scale.

Military Retirement Facts as of 2012

1. In order to receive a 'tax-free' retirement you must qualify for a combat related disability.
2. You only receive one paycheck a month; as opposed to your current bi-monthly payments.
3. First payment will be 30 days after your retirement date; you will receive this on the first business day of each month.
4. Retirement pay can be garnished for alimony, child support, IRS tax levies and debts owed to the government (i.e. student loans).

5. Divorce—Under provisions of the Uniformed Services Former Spouse Protection Act, state courts may treat military retired pay as joint property.
6. Cost of Living Adjustments (COLA) are given annually based on the increase in the Consumer Price Index (CPI), a measure of inflation.

*Active Duty Base Salary		Retirement Income Value	
E-8	**O-5**	**E-8**	**O-5**
Monthly Salary	Monthly Salary	Monthly Salary	Monthly Salary
$4,767	$8,199	$2,383	$4,099
Annual Salary	Annual Salary	Annual Salary	Annual Salary
$57,204	$98,388	$28,596	$49,188

Note: This amount excludes housing/subsistence and extra pay allowances and is pre-tax dollars.

Lifetime Value of Military Retirement*	
E-8	**O-5**
Retirement for 20 Years	Retirement for 20 Years
$571,920	$983,760

*Note: The average life expectancy is 77, thus the average Soldier will receive the above benefits up to 35 years (Officer) and 37 years (Enlisted), which results in a number twice as big as the 20 year retirement values above.

(Default) High-3 Retirement System

This system applies to those individuals who entered on or after 1 August 1986, who did not elect the REDUX retirement system with the Career Status Bonus (CSB) at their 15th year of service. This is the 'classic model' 2.5% for each year of service (20 years x 2.5%= 50% base pay).

*Reference the website, **www.militarypay.defense.gov**, for updated facts and tools to help you plan for your military retirement.*

Career Status Bonus (CSB)/REDUX (Must elect)

Applies to those that entered the service on or after 1 August, 1986, AND who elected to receive the **$30,000 Career Status Bonus (CSB)** at their 15th year of service. The CSB and REDUX retirement system is a package deal. The REDUX portion determines the retirement income (the longer one's

E-8 Monthly Base Salary $4,767

Years in Service	CSB (3.5%)	High-3 Retirement (2.5%)	Monthly Difference	Yearly Difference
20 Yrs	$1,907	$2,383	$476	$5,712
23 Yrs	$2,407	$2,741	$334	$4,008
27 Yrs	$3,075	$3,218	$143	$1,716
30 Yrs	$3,575	$3,575	$0	$0

O-5 Monthly Base Salary $8,199

Years in Service	CSB (3.5%)	High-3 Retirement (2.5%)	Monthly Difference	Yearly Difference
20 Yrs	$3,279	$4,099	$476	$5,712
23 Yrs	$4,140	$4,714	$334	$4,008
27 Yrs	$5,288	$5,534	$143	$1,716
30 Yrs	$6,149	$6,149	$0	$0

career, the higher that income) and **the $30,000 CSB provides cash**. The first **20 years of service is only worth 2% per year (20 years x 2%=40% base pay)**. However, each year **after 20 the Soldier receives 3.5% per year; basically if you serve for the 30 years you will match the High-3 system and you will receive a CSB that your peers didn't receive in the High-3 system.**

1. **$30,000 CSB**—Must elect at 15th year of service. Member must agree to complete a 20 year active duty career. It comes to about $21,000 after taxes.
    a. Reference **www.militarypay.defense.gov/retirement** for more details.
2. Keep DFAS apprised of any changes in personal information at **www.dfas.mil** or 1-800-321-1080.

Medical Benefits/TRICARE

Retired Soldiers and their families are still entitled to TRICARE benefits including dental insurance. If the Soldier chooses TRICARE Standard, there are **no monthly** or annual premiums, but you are subject to co-pay and deductibles. If the Soldier chooses TRICARE Prime there is an **annual enrollment fee** that can be paid annually, quarterly or monthly. This fee can also be set up as an allotment from retirement pay. It is typically less than $40/month for family coverage. Reference **www.tricare.mil** for more information.

Note: Dental insurance can be set up on an allotment as well. The amount varies based on the type of coverage but it is considerably more than active duty premiums.

In 2012, although it depends on which region of the country you live in, you can expect to pay on average $230 per year for individual coverage or $460 per year for family coverage under TRICARE Prime. To put this in perspective, in the civilian market, according to the Kaiser Family Foundation's Survey of Employer-Sponsored Health Benefits for 1999-2009, the average annual cost of health care is $4,824 for an individual and $13,375 for a family. When compared to civilian costs, you can quickly see the value of TRICARE insurance upon retirement.

Type and Duration	Commercial Cost	Comparative Health Insurance Costs TRICARE	Savings
Individual 20 Years ($4,824)	$96,480	$4,600	$91,880
Individual 30 Years ($4,824)	$144,720	$6,900	$137,820
Family 20 Years ($13,375)	$267,500	$9,200	$258,300
Family 30 Years ($13,375)	$401,250	$13,800	$387,450

Final Note

It is recommended by many financial professionals that for any retirement strategy you begin sooner rather than later. Even if you can only invest a small amount to start, the sooner you develop your retirement strategy the better off you will probably be. There are hidden costs to retirement, such as medical insurance. Think about the advantages and savings that retiring from the military earns you when considering your retirement strategy. As with everything, do your research before selecting any investment strategy.

Only two things are guaranteed... death and taxes.

—*Benjamin Franklin*
Patriot

Taxes

BLUF:
The government has made paying and reporting taxes easy for Soldiers, but knowing the system can put more money in your pocket.
• Taxable Income
• Combat Zone Exclusions
• Tax Deductible Expenses

Discussion:
This section will cover some of the main areas of the 'special tax considerations' of active duty members in the U.S. Army. You can reference IRS Publication 910 if you need a list of the other IRS materials.

Who Does the IRS Consider Military?
The IRS recognizes those commissioned officers, warrant officers, and enlisted personnel under the control of the Secretary of Defense as being "military". As a member of the U.S. Army (Active, Reserve and National Guard) you are covered.

Gross Income
Gross income is a Soldier's income before taking taxes or deductions into account. The Leave and Earnings Statement (LES) shows your gross income in the "Entitlements" section.

The sample LES shows base pay, basic allowance for subsistence (BAS), and basic allowance for housing (BAH) included in the average Soldier's entitlements. If you have never seen your LES, here is an example of what you are looking for.

Example Leave and Earnings Statement

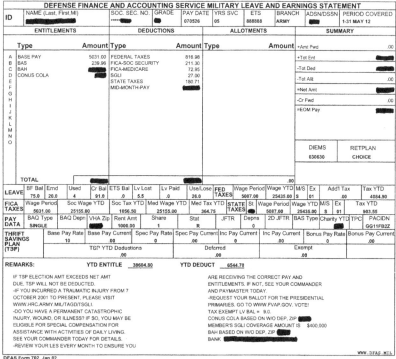

There are a broad range of entitlements. Some of these entitlements are subject to tax, must be reported on your tax return, and are referred to as "Included Items." **The items below become "tax exempt" when serving in a combat zone.**

Excluded Items

The other category of income for the American Soldier is Excluded Income. Excluded items **are not subject to tax**, but may have to be shown on your tax return.

Exempted Items

Basic Pay	Special Pay	Bonus Pay
• Active Duty Pay • Attendance at service school • Back wages • CONUS Cost of Living • Drills • Reserve Training	• Foreign language proficiency • Hardship duty • Hostile fire • Aviation incentives	• Reenlistment/ Enlistment

Excluded Items

Living Allowance	• BAH and BAS
Travel Allowance	• Annual round trip for dependent students • Leave between consecutive overseas tours • Per diem • Student loan repayment programs
Moving Allowance	• Dislocation • Move-in housing • Storage • Temporary lodging and associated expenses
Combat Zone Pay	• Compensation for active service while in a combat zone
Other Pay	• Defense counseling • Disability, including payments received for injuries incurred as a direct result of terrorist or military action • Group-term life insurance • ROTC education and subsistence allowances • State bonus pay for service in a combat zone • Survivor and retirement protection plan premiums • Uniform allowances

Combat Zone Exclusions

As a member of the Army serving in a combat zone, certain income is excluded from certain taxes. **A combat zone is an area designated by the President of the United States through an Executive Order as an area where the Army is engaged in combat.**

The month in which you receive the tax-free pay must be the month that you either served in a combat zone or were hospitalized due to injuries sustained in a combat zone. If you serve in a combat zone for any part of a month, you are entitled to tax-free income for that month, as of 2011. For 2012, you will only receive tax-free benefits for the days that you were in a combat zone, not for the entire month, rounded up.

Combat Zone Tax-Free Money

- Active duty pay earned in combat zone
- Imminent danger/hostile fire pay
- Reenlistment bonuses if voluntary extension occurs in month you served in a combat zone
- Pay accrued leave earned in any month you served in a combat zone
- Student loan repayments
- Awards for suggestions, inventions, or scientific achievements submitted while in combat

Combat Zone Actions That Don't Earn Tax-Free

- Presence in a combat zone while on leave
- Passage over or through a combat zone during a trip between two points
- Presence in a combat zone solely for your personal convenience

Areas Designated as a Combat Zone in 2012

- Afghanistan Combat Zone (Operation Enduring Freedom)
- Former Yugoslavia
- Albania
- Arabian Peninsula Areas (Operation Iraqi Freedom)

Sale of Home
You may not have to pay tax on the gain from the sale of your main home, which can be a house, houseboat, mobile home or condo. If this residence is your primary residence, **you can generally exclude up to $250,000 ($500,000 if married filing jointly) of gain realized on that home's sale.** You can do this each time you sell or exchange a main home. For a home to be defined as your "primary home" you must have owned the home for at least two years. A PCS move allows for the exception to the "primary home" test. Consult JAG for specific instructions.

Standard Deduction
A standard deduction is a dollar amount that reduces the amount of income on which you are taxed. You can default to a standard deduction if you do not have more itemized deductions than your standard deduction. Refer to **www.irs.gov** for your current standard deduction amount.

You may not have to pay tax on the gain from the sale of your main home.

Itemized Deductions
An itemized deduction is a deduction from your adjusted gross income that is made up of deductions for money spent on certain goods and services throughout the year.

Travel Expenses
Unreimbursed travel expenses can be deducted if incurred while on work-related business. You cannot deduct expenses accumulated while on leave or while at your permanent duty station. An example of such are expenses accumulated while carrying out official business while on "No Cost" orders.

Transportation Expenses
If you go from one workplace to another while on duty without being away from home, your unreimbursed transportation expenses are deductible. For example, as a courier, attending meetings or traveling to conduct a funeral, all unreimbursed expenses are deductible.

Forgiveness of Dependent's Tax Liability

Tax liability can be forgiven if a member of the Army dies. The IRS will determine the amount eligible for forgiveness. *Liability is forgiven for Soldiers that are killed in a combat zone.*

Filing Returns

This section outlines the special procedures for military personnel when filing federal taxes.

Where to File

Although filing tax returns on paper is a well-known traditional method, filing online is quicker, and typically more accurate because of the step-by-step process of the online service. It is often much less expensive than going to a professional accountant. Tax filing sites, such as **www.taxslayer.com/military** provide Soldiers with a **free tax filing service.** These services also track all of your past returns, reducing the risk of lost paperwork from previous year's returns. In addition, many posts set up tax filing centers to assist Soldiers. Operated by and under the direction of JAG officers, these centers provide Soldiers with a comprehensive tax filing service that is free of charge.

Your post's JAG office is designed to provide general legal assistance.

When to File

The **due date for filing taxes is April 15th.** As a Soldier you are eligible for an extension on the filing date; but be aware that you will be charged interest on any money owed to the federal government. If serving in a combat zone, the IRS automatically extends your filing deadline. The extension is typically 180 days after the last day of your combat zone tour or the last day of a qualified hospital stay resulting from a combat zone injury.

FREE Tax Help

In addition to your post's tax center, there are numerous other resources to get free tax assistance. Free help is available nationwide through the Volunteer Income Tax Assistance program, which is designed to help low to moderate income taxpayers. **Additionally, your post's JAG office is designed to provide general legal assistance.**

Some Soldiers may qualify for participation in the Low Income Taxpayer Clinic (LITCs). LITCs are independent from the IRS, yet they provide professional representation for the IRS. For more information visit **www.irs. gov/advocate.**

Final Note

Like it or not, taxes are part of your life as an American. As a Soldier there are many systems in place to reduce the burden taxes place on you and your family. Take advantage of these systems.

A bank is a place that will lend you money if you can prove that you don't need it.

—*Bob Hope*
Comedian

Credit

BLUF:
Credit is the ability to obtain goods or services before payment, based on the trust that payment will be made in the future.
• How to build it.
• How credit works for you.

Discussion:
Credit is complex, so let's focus on what it means to you. Credit can play a positive or negative role in your life and it is in your interest to understand the fundamentals of credit. The four most common times that your credit will be checked is when dealing with: (1) insurance companies (2) landlords (3) employers (4) home or auto purchase. Credit is a powerful tool that, if used correctly, can open up doors to your future.

What is a Credit Score?
A credit score is a number expressing a person's credit-worthiness used by lenders to access the likelihood that a person will repay his or her debts. There are a multitude of ways to check your credit score, but the key is to check one of the three credit reporting agencies: Equifax, Trans Union, and Experian—which you can do *once a year for free*. (**www.annualcreditreport. com**). You do not want to wait until

FICO Credit Score	Percent of Americans
*800-850	13
*760-799	27
700-759	18
650-699	15
600-649	12
550-599	8
500-549	5

*Top Tier-These are the scores that will receive the best interest rates. Below 760, you are considered higher risk, and the interest you will be charged will be higher.

a "lender" checks your credit; there are times when mistakes are made on your credit report, and even after they are identified, it can take months

A good credit score is critical: the higher your score, the less you pay to borrow money.

to fix. Be proactive and avoid the frustration and embarrassment of an inaccurately reported credit history by checking your credit score annually.

The highest possible credit score is 850, while the lowest is 300. The score is critical because the higher your score, the less you pay to borrow money. Most lenders require a score of at least 760 in order to get the best interest rates. Below 760, mortgage rates increase according to these score brackets: 700-759, 660-699, 620-659, 580-619, and 500-579. Interest rates increase significantly with a score below 620, because at this point, lenders consider you to be in the subprime category: you will be charged more to borrow because you are considered a poor risk for repaying your debt.

Credit in Everyday Life

Insurance
Both auto and homeowner's insurance agencies perform credit checks before determining the rate that they will offer you. Statistics show that drivers with a lower tier credit score file 40% more claims.

Rental Property
Landlords take a look at a multitude of things before they commit to signing a lease with a tenant and one of the most important is the tenant's credit report. If you have bad credit, the landlord typically asks for a larger security deposit; security deposits, if you have good credit, typically amount to one month's rent, paid during lease signing in addition to the first and last month's rent; for a typical total initial payment of three month's rent at signing.

Home Purchase
The difference between having a credit score of 760 and a mediocre score of 579 results in the following: with a rate of 760 if you borrow $300k to purchase a house, and it is a 30-year fixed-rate mortgage, you would save $600 each month / $7,000 each year / $210,000 over the life of the loan. You are getting a lower interest rate with a 760 credit score and are

therefore paying considerably less money, in interest, each time that you make a payment. The longer the period of the loan, the more money you will save by having a higher credit score. The bank will approve you for a lower interest rate because you are considered to be a "lower risk." Numbers do not lie, and this example displays the obvious: a good credit score gives you great security, flexibility and potentially can save you hundreds of thousands of dollars in interest.

Credit Score Comparison	760	579
Loan Amount	$300,000	$300,000
Interest Rate	6.925%	9.925%
Length of Loan	30 years	30 years
Monthly Payments	$1,980	$2,616
Annual Payment	$23,760	$31,392
Annual Difference	$7,632	
Life of Loan (30 Years) Difference	$228,960	

Employers
Employers have been known to do credit checks on potential employees. The idea is simple: if you are not responsible enough to pay your bills and live within your means, how can you be expected to arrive at work on-time or balance a budget within your prospective organization?

You have to "use" credit in order to build it. The most common example is getting a major credit card and *paying your entire balance in full each month.*

Security Clearance

If you are applying for a Top Secret Security Clearance you can expect a credit check to be conducted. The government wants to make sure that sensitive information is not shared with someone that might be under extreme financial pressure, and therefore potentially susceptible to bribes.

What Affects Your Credit?

1. Bank Accounts—You do not need credit to establish a checking account, but your account history could be a vital component when lenders consider giving you a credit card or a loan for the first time.
2. Employment History—Demonstrate that you have steady employment. Longer employment shows a steady paycheck and demonstrates to the lender that you are more likely to make payments on time.
3. Residence History—Being stable in the same location and renting or owning (apartment, house, etc.) can influence first time borrower's chances of being approved for a loan.

Building Credit

1. **Get credit.** You have to "use" credit in order to build it. The most common example is getting a major credit card and *paying your entire balance in full each month.* Consider getting a credit card with a reputable firm, such as USAA Savings Bank or one that fits your needs such as one that gives you extra bonuses every time you use it at a grocery store or where you earn air miles for dollars spent. (Be very careful of credit card or loan offers advertising "0% down and 0% percent interest.") *Note—this can often be a buyer's trap; lenders give you great deals in the beginning, only to quickly raise the rates. Shop around for cards with permanently low interest rates.*

What Affects Your Credit Score		
Affect	**Weight**	**Remarks**
Payment History	35%	1. When was your last default on payment? 2. How many payments did you miss?
Current Credit Situation	30%	The amount that you are currently financing; most Americans only use 30% of their available credit.
Length of Credit History	15%	The longer that you have established a line of credit the better.
Application for Credit	10%	It's a red flag to financiers if you have had multiple credit checks in a short period of time; comes across that you are desperate for money.
Types of Credit	10%	Two types; Revolving (credit cards) and Installment (mortgages/car loans).

2. **Be patient.** None of this happens overnight, but similar to most things in this book, it is strongly suggested that you begin building credit early. The time that it takes for you to build good credit depends on a number of factors, but it generally takes several years.
3. **Be consistent.** Make payments on time.

Final Note

People who do not pay their bills are considered to have more risk in their lives. Credit can affect your life in both obvious and unforeseen ways. A bad credit rating—which can be easily avoided—can cost you and your family thousands of dollars over the life of various necessary loans.

In God we trust;
all others must pay cash.

—American Proverb

Debt

BLUF:
When we think about debt, many of us immediately assume that it is always bad, when in fact, debt can be used to our advantage.
- Good vs. bad debt
- How to get out of debt
- Tips and tricks to managing debt

Discussion:
Depending upon your situation, debt can either be good or bad. A rule of thumb: view debt as an **investment in the future worth** of the item being purchased. If the item will not be around long enough to have a future value, then it should probably not be purchased with debt (a loan). For example, a dependable used car purchased using a low interest rate loan for "daily use" is a good use of debt because your future livelihood (i.e. getting to work, taking the kids to school, doctor's appointments, etc.) depends on having that car. A quick example of bad debt is putting a $200 pair of shoes on a credit card when you don't have the cash to immediately pay off that card's balance at the end of month. Those shoes may look good, but they won't help you pay your bill when the credit card interest gets tacked onto the $200. Below are a few other common examples of typically good and bad debt.

Bad Debt	Good Debt
• Payday Loan	• Mortgage
• Borrowing against Retirement (TSP)	• Student Loan
• Credit Card	• Credit Cards (paid off monthly)
• Auto Loan (New)	• Auto Loan (Used)

Bad Debt

Payday Loan

Payday loans—sometimes referred to as short-term loans—are the worst kind of debt to assume because you will be charged an extremely high amount of interest. A typical payday loan scenario illustrates how this type of loan takes advantage of Soldiers: borrow $325 and the average payday loan could ultimately cost you a total of $793—an interest rate of about **140%** over the course of the payback period. This particularly hurts because as a Soldier you have numerous "interest free" alternatives.

When Soldiers cannot repay the excessive amount the lender is quick to extend the debt and deduct the full loan amount, plus additional fees, when the Soldier's next paycheck is direct deposited. And thus your original debt quadruples. **Eighteen states have banned payday loans in order to protect Soldiers and citizens.**

Army Emergency Relief (AER) provides Soldiers with an alternative! AER is "the Army's own emergency financial assistance organization" designed to provide interest-free loans to Soldiers in need. Ultimately, Soldiers must repay the loan, but the loan gives Soldiers a better option, and prevents them from turning to short term lenders in order to secure basic household goods, vehicles, etc. Your commander is typically the approving authority for an AER loan. Ask your chain of command or go to **www.aerhq.org** for more information.

> **Army Emergency Relief is "the Army's own emergency financial assistance organization" designed to provide interest-free loans.**

Credit Card

You should understand that credit card interest rates are high. According to **www.indexcreditcards.com**, the current average consumer credit card interest rate is 16.70%. But credit cards are also extremely convenient. With a credit card handy you can spend a great deal of money on everyday consumer items like clothing or food. When the amount that you spend exceeds the amount you are actually able to repay by the end of the month, you not only purchased the initial item, you now also owe the associated interest (i.e. item price + 16.70%). Most credit cards attempt to exploit a person's tendency to overspend because this is one of the ways credit card agencies make their money. However, by staying within your means and using credit cards to purchase items you can afford it's possible stay on top of expenses and build a solid credit rating. Avoid overspending and you will avoid excessive interest rates and penalties, keeping your hard-earned money for yourself.

The average credit card debt per American consumer is $5,650.

–Jenna Herron Contributor at Bankrate.com

Withdrawing and Borrowing from Retirement

Avoid withdrawing from your retirement accounts because there are often high penalties for using your money before the age of 59½ and the power of compounding interest greatly decreases when you remove your principal (refer to the Retirement chapter for details). Even though you can also borrow from your TSP, you are defeating the purpose of keeping your money inside the TSP so it is available later in your life.

Auto Loan (New)

Auto loans for new cars fall into the bad debt category. According to Edmunds.com, **as soon as you drive a new car off the lot, it loses more than 10% of its value**: a $30,000 car loses $3,339. This means that the moment you drive your new car away, you instantly owe more on the car than it is worth. Here's the worst case scenario: you took out a $30,000 loan to pay for your new truck, but that vehicle is immediately worth $26,661. And you still owe $30,000. You never want to take out a loan that exceeds the value of your purchase.

Good Debt

Home Mortgage

Most people who purchase a home do so with credit. The good news is that there is the possibility, over time, of appreciation in the value of your home and a large percentage of your mortgage is tax deductible (refer to the Taxes chapter). This means that unlike the new car that immediately depreciates as soon as it is driven off the lot, your home's value has the potential to increase in value the longer you own it.

But being in the military, home buying can be a double-edged sword: although homes can appreciate, that happens in cycles. Some years there is a decrease in overall home values, and today's real estate market is the perfect example. Because Soldiers PCS approximately every three years, this makes us more susceptible to the housing market's uncertainty (refer to the Home Purchase section for more information). Generally speaking, a home can still be a good investment for those Soldiers who can afford it and who expect to be at one duty station for an extended period of time.

Student Loan

Student debt should be viewed as an investment in yourself. The more education you have, the faster you will be promoted in the Army and the more money you will earn. Refer to the chapter on Education. Soldiers have a wealth of cost-free educational benefits so you may not have to spend money or take on debt to gain a higher level of education. However if you ultimately have to invest in your education it will likely pay dividends in the future.

Student debt should be viewed as an investment in yourself.

Credit Cards

If you can pay back the full credit card balance at the end of each month, then some credit cards can prove more beneficial to your overall finances than traditional cash spending. Many credit cards offer some type of rewards program to "incentivize" consumers selecting their card over the dozens of major credit card competitors. These rewards can range from air miles to cash back on every dollar spent. Ironically, these credit cards often give out the rewards even though you pay off your balance at the end of the month. For Soldiers who can control spending and **pay their entire bill "in full" every month**, you reap the rewards of all the incentives without paying any of those steep interest rates.

Note—credit cards carry higher interest rates and penalize people that cannot or choose not to pay their bill in full each month.

Selecting a Credit Card
• No annual fees
• User friendly website/customer service
• Compare rewards (**www.creditcardguide.com**)
• Interest rates (**Hint**: Interest rate charges are largely avoided if you can pay off your entire credit card bill at the end of each month.)

Managing Credit Card Debt
1. **Develop a good tracking system.** Write down your entire debt. Compare your debt with interest rates, length of debt, total amount, and any tax advantages associated with that debt.
2. **Negotiate interest rates.** Nearly every credit card's interest rate is negotiable. If you find yourself with credit card debt, call the credit card company and ask them to lower your current rate.
3. **Strategize paying off existing debt.** Use your extra cash to pay off the credit card with the highest interest rate; when that balance is paid off, focus your cash on the card with the next highest rate, and so on.

Auto Loan (Used)
Recognizing that a car depreciates quickly, it is best to let another buyer absorb the initial value loss. You can still get the car you want—and save a lot of money—by allowing someone else to drive it off the lot first: buy a used car. You will have to do some research to find when these types of gently used (pre-owned, rented, certified, etc.) cars come up for sale. When you find the used car that you want to purchase, do some research on the Internet to be sure that you are getting the best price and the lowest interest rate. View your car as a means of transportation and not an extension of

Paying off debt is a simple concept, but there are certain strategies that are better than others.

your ego. Your investment should be worth at least as much as the debt that you incur.

Home Equity Loans

Be cautious when borrowing against the "equity" in your home. If you have a property that is valued at $300,000 and you owe $100,000 on your mortgage, your equity is $200,000. Home equity loans and lines of credit are some of the ways that homeowners can borrow money using their home's value as collateral. Home equity products are relatively low-cost ways to borrow money, but they must be repaid like any other loan and interest rates on these types of loans are usually adjustable and will fluctuate up and down with the market. Remember if you cannot make your payments on a home equity loan, you risk losing your home. **Home equity interest is a deductible expense under many circumstances when you are preparing your taxes.**

Final Note

Pay Your Debt: Paying off debt is a simple concept, but there are certain strategies that are better than others. (1) Analyze which debts have the highest interest rate. These are the debts that are costing you the most money in interest every year. (2) Is my debt "good" debt, i.e. mortgage or education or "bad" debt, i.e. new trendy wardrobe or collector items bought on credit?

*Predatory lending
is a cancer that should
be wiped out.*

—Keith Ernst
Center for Responsible Lending

Predatory Lending

BLUF:
Learn to recognize the signs of predatory lending practices and protect yourself from it.

Discussion:
A predatory loan benefits the lender at the borrower's expense. In the case of a mortgage loan, there might be above-average fees, excessive or unnecessary fees, or overly high interest rates that prevent the borrower from accumulating home equity. A lender convincing a borrower to refinance or take out a home equity loan when there is little to no benefit to the borrower, or might prove harmful also can be considered predatory.

Common Red Flags for Predatory Loans
- Interest rate appears too good to be true
- Pressure is applied to act quickly
- Fees are higher than the competition
- Rates suddenly change during "closing"

Note: *An excellent reference for the latest Tactics, Techniques and Procedures (TTPs) of predatory loans is* **www.responsiblelending.org**.

Signs of Predatory Lending

Mortgages
- **Soldiers with bad credit beware.** Always avoid lenders or brokers who contact you or try to rush you into decisions. Predatory lenders also often target senior citizens and other financially vulnerable people to place them in unnecessarily expensive loans.
- Estimates of mortgage payments that include only the interest and principal, but do not include property taxes and homeowners' insurance, can be signs of predatory practices. Know, in advance, if your monthly mortgage payment will include the costs of property taxes and insurance, or if you will pay those costs separately.

- Adjustable Rate Mortgage (ARM): Ask and understand exactly how high the rate can adjust during each adjustment period, and over the life of the loan. The initial rate of the ARM may seem like a bargain, but you can safely assume that when the time for adjustment arrives, a lender that is predatory (and certainly not all are) will seek to make up for the difference with increased interest rates that could dramatically increase the amount of your monthly mortgage payment.

Credit/Debit Cards

- **Print changes:** Credit card companies make big changes in small print, especially with respect to interest rate increases. Always review both the initial terms, as well as the initial conditions of your credit card, followed by a careful review of any materials received with each monthly statement.
- **Fees:** Credit card regulations have been significantly overhauled, largely in order to insure that issuers specify and enumerate disclosures. In addition to cash advance and balance transfer fees, credit card companies are adding inactivity fees, statement fees, foreign currency fees and other miscellaneous surcharges.
- **Payment protection:** Credit card issuers will routinely attempt to sell you payment protection, identity theft protection, credit monitoring services, or other products. They can make more money in the sale of these services. Watch out for quotes in terms of pennies per $1 used to make the price appear low. Be cautious of "free trial period deals." If you forget to cancel when the period expires, the chances are good that you will be automatically renewed, for a fee.
- **Credit card policies:** Stop credit card and debit card issuers from charging fees when you go over your credit limit, unless you specifically authorize the company to do so. However, when the issuer does cover your overdraft expense, you will incur a fee as high as $35 for an overdraft charge that might have only been in the amount of a few dollars. Some companies have begun to make "deceptive calls" in an attempt to pressure customers to buy into their respective credit card overdraft system. Consider not buying into this system, and instead set up your savings account or similar account to automatically cover any overdraft. The best-case scenario is to be frugal, and maintain a running balance of your credit and debit cards, which can be attached to your checking account to insure you don't go over your limit.

Auto Loans

- **Situation:** At the dealership, a car buyer initially qualifies for a lower interest rate or a "buy rate." The dealer has a powerful incentive to increase the interest rate, because most of the extra interest accrued is "kicked back" to the dealer. Dealer loans are often more expensive than you can find elsewhere.
- **Inflate price:** Dealers often increase the price of a car loan through unnecessary add-ons that are sold in packages. Add-ons include vehicle service contracts, credit life and disability insurance, rust proofing, and theft deterrent packages. Dealers that inflate the vehicle's cost and loan size, in turn receive a larger "kick back."

> Situation: At the dealership, anyone offering you "quick cash" or an "unbeatable deal" should be looked at closely.

Car Title Loans

- **Car title loans:** One of the most common predatory lending scams involves short term "payday" loans that use your car as collateral. If you fail to pay off your loan, you lose your car. Most car title loans are due within a month. The short term loan period makes it much more difficult to pay off your loan in time, thereby forcing you to miss loan payments, which results in penalties, increased interest accruement, and loss of title, property, etc. In Missouri, the state auditor found that car title lenders make 3.5 times more on renewal loans than on new loans each month.
- **Car title lenders** often express the cost of the loan as a fee, but a typical car title loan may have a high annual interest rate of up to **three times the market rate.**

Final Note

Anyone offering you "quick cash" or an "unbeatable deal" should be looked at closely. As a Soldier you have access to all sorts of emergency loans (furniture, money, etc). Don't fall prey to super high interest rates. Ask questions and don't rush into any contract without knowing how much it will ultimately cost you.

Investing should be more like watching paint dry or watching grass grow. If you want excitement, take $800 and go to Las Vegas.

Paul Samuelson
Investor

Investments

BLUF:
This chapter will provide a basic explanation of some investing options and a short synopsis of some viable investments to consider.

Investments FDIC insured	Investments NOT FDIC insured
• Savings Account • Money Market Deposit Account • Certificates of Deposit (CD)	• Treasury Securities • Mutual Funds • Stocks

Discussion:
There are a large number of financial vehicles to choose from and your initial investigation, either through the Internet, a close friend, or your financial advisor, can be extremely intimidating. The end state of this chapter is to give you an understanding of some of the different investment options for you to use in your Roth IRA or Traditional IRA, after you have funded your emergency savings account. There are many options to choose from, but the first and most important step is gaining a fundamental understanding of the risk and reward associated with each. **Any time an investment is offering a higher return, you must consider that there is a higher risk involved, and a higher likelihood of losing your money.**

FDIC Insurance Coverage:
Federal Deposit Insurance Corporation (FDIC) accounts are fully protected by the federal government if your bank fails. The basic insurance coverage is $250,000 per depositor per insured institution. Anything that is backed by the FDIC is extremely secure.

1. **Savings Account**—FDIC insured. An account used to deposit money at a bank or credit union. Very flexible, safe and (currently) has a low interest rate.

2. **Money Market Deposit Account**—FDIC insured (dependent on the financial institution). A savings account that typically offers a higher rate of interest in exchange for larger than normal deposits. (The more commonly used Money Market Mutual Funds are described below and are not FDIC insured.)

3. **Certificates of Deposit (CD)**—FDIC insured. A savings certificate entitling the bearer to receive interest on that amount. A CD has a maturity date, a specific interest rate, and can be issued in any denomination, but places restrictions on when money can be taken out.

4. **Treasury Securities**—When purchasing a treasury security, you loan your money to the government. In return, you are paid interest on your loan and the face value of the bond at maturity.

5. **Mutual Fund**—Professionally managed funds invested in a variety of stocks or bonds, in part to spread the risk of loss from any one company's poor performance. This investment is made up of money collected by many investors for the purpose of investing primarily in individual stocks and individual bonds. An **Index Fund** is a type of mutual fund with a portfolio that matches components and the performance of a particular market index, the Standard and Poor's 500 Index, for example.

6. **Stocks**—Give you ownership or a "share" of a company. Stock prices move up and down based on the perception of investors about how well the company and its industry are doing, how high they think the stock price may go, etc. The Law of Supply vs Demand applies: if more investors want to buy shares than sell shares, the price will generally go up. If more investors want to sell shares than buy shares, the price will generally go down.

Investing

The financial world is large and confusing. Consulting a financial advisor or one of the JAG supported offices is critical to fully understanding your investment options. You know that you want to save and be financially secure when you retire, but the first question everyone has is, "Where do I put the money that I have saved?"

There is advice that is available and will help you make your money work harder for you. Investing in a savings account or a CD is safe and FDIC-insured, but perhaps not as efficient in terms of earnings or taxes over the long term.

As far as options other than a traditional savings account or CD, there are hundreds of financial institutions and thousands of mutual funds to choose from. You may be thinking, "I just want to put my money in a place that is safe, but still be able to gain a return on my initial investment." Remember, not every financial vehicle is going to earn a 10% rate of return or even a 2% return, but every financial vehicle that you choose needs to fall into a category that fits your financial plan and your lifestyle. For example, when you set up your emergency savings fund, if you want the money to be safe, guaranteed, and not subject to stock market risk, then that narrows the number of options that fit your needs.

Consulting a financial advisor is critical to fully understanding your investment options.

Investment Priorities

1. Emergency Savings: two to three months' easily accessible money
2. Retirement
3. Tax Advantages
4. Future Purchase (house or auto)
5. Education
6. Personal Net Worth

Savings and Money Market Deposit Accounts (Emergency Savings or Future Purchase)

Savings and Money Market Deposit Accounts are some safe ways to manage *liquid assets* (cash). You never know when you might need some money and a "shoe-box" under the bed just isn't the investment vehicle it used to be.

Savings Account

Advantages:

- Risk-free way to put money aside (up to $250,000 FDIC-insured)
- Unlimited access—use money whenever you need it. Some banks may place a two to three day hold upon withdrawal requests, but many banks do not (unless the amount is particularly large)
- Online banking

Note: Online savings accounts give the highest rates of return, usually competitive with money market deposit accounts (covered by the FDIC). They have a higher yield, because they don't have the cost of the 'brick and mortar' banks, thus you benefit in the return by getting a higher interest rate.

Disadvantages:

- Traditionally lowest annual rate of return out of all listed investment types
- Earnings are taxed
- Sometimes have minimum balances—which varies
- Some fees may exist

Money Market Deposit Account

Advantages:

- Tiered interest rates—the more money in the account, the higher the rate of return
- FDIC insured up to $250,000—**one of the highest rates of return for FDIC-insured investments**

Disadvantages:

- High minimum balances—between $500 and $5,000
- **Limited to three withdrawals per month**—less liquid than savings account
- Some are associated with monthly fees
- Interest rate fluctuation—subject to market conditions

Certificate of Deposit and Treasury Securities
(Emergency Savings and Saving for Future Purchases)
Certificates of Deposits (CDs) and Treasury notes and bonds earn a pre-determined interest rate. Both categories are relatively low risk investments whose interest rates depend on the market, at the time of investment.

Certificates of Deposit
A CD is an investment with a bank that typically offers a higher rate of interest than a savings account. If you choose to purchase a CD you are agreeing to leave your money in the bank for a set amount of time and in exchange you will receive a pre-determined rate of return. To put it another way, on the first day of the investment, you generally know exactly how much profit you will earn at maturity. There are some exceptions to this basic type of CD, but do your research to determine the exact type of CD you are investing in. Generally, the longer the CD takes to mature the higher the interest rate.

Generally, the longer the CD takes to mature the higher the interest rate.

Advantages:
• Secure investment backed by FDIC
• Competitive interest rates publicized prior to investment
• Invest "X" amount today, get "Y" amount in the future

Disadvantages:
• Typically, you cannot get to your money in an emergency without paying a heavy penalty
• Rigid interest rates that do not increase during bull markets (bull markets = good market)
• Earnings are taxed if the CD is held by you as an individual rather than in something like an IRA

Treasury Securities
Treasury securities are a broad set of investment vehicles. Generally speaking, all of these investments are US government debt securities. These

securities differ in the length of time that each takes to expire, as well as the respective interest rates. Usually, the longer the investment takes to expire, the higher the rate of return. Each type has its own features, advantages, and interest formulas.

Advantages:

- Secure investment backed **by the full faith and credit of the US government (although not FDIC).**
- Some types of securities are exempt from state and local taxes
- Can purchase certain securities directly from the US government at **www.savingsbonds.gov**

Disadvantages:

- Low yield to maturity when compared to other investments (these investments are in great demand because of their safety, so the US Treasury does not pay a high interest rate)
- Sensitive to political risk. How the world perceives the United States government's stability directly affects Treasury Security return rates

Treasury Bill

Short-term investment that expires in one year or less. These are sold at a discount from their face value (par). Ex: You buy a $10,000 T-Bill for $9,900, and get $10,000 at maturity.

Treasury Note

Medium-term investment expires in two to ten years; interest rates don't change. Owners of Treasury notes receive interest payments every six months.

Treasury Bond

Long-term investments; expires in 10 years or more. A Treasury bond pays interest every six months until it matures. Interest rates slightly change throughout the life of the bond. When a Treasury bond matures, you are paid its face value.

I Bond

Rates include a fixed rate set at the time of purchase for the 30-year life of the bond, plus an inflation adjustment that changes to reflect inflation.

Mutual Funds

It has already been established that opening an IRA is an important financial step in securing a financial future. A mutual fund is an investment that you can put into your Roth IRA or Traditional IRA that allows you to invest in a number of stocks and bonds without taking the risk of investing in a single stock or a single bond. They can be purchased directly through a mutual fund company, through brokerage firms, insurance companies, banks, etc. Three things you should know about a mutual fund:

1. **Defined:** A mutual fund is an investment vehicle that compiles money from different people or resources and is invested in a number of individual stocks and bonds. Mutual funds are managed with the intent of achieving a specific investment objective such as long-term growth of capital, high rate of current income, tax-free income, etc; or the fund could have a specific area that it invests in such as precious metals, real estate, international markets, environmentally conscious companies, etc.

2. **Diversification and management:** A mutual fund portfolio is allocated among a number of different stocks and bonds in order to diversify your risk, and the mutual fund manager is paid to achieve the objective set out in the prospectus. **Morningstar.com** is an excellent resource for evaluating mutual funds.

3. **Fees:** A mutual fund requires you to pay fees so the owners and managers of the firm make money. Be conscious of the annual costs of holding mutual funds, and review those costs within the overall context of how the fund is performing. Some mutual funds are "Load" funds: commissions are assessed at the time of purchase of a mutual fund. There are

> **Historically, the S&P 500 has returned 10.8%, disregarding inflation, since its inception in 1957. However, it's important to note that investment markets are volatile and have experienced many years where there have been dramatic losses.**

also thousands of "No-Load" mutual funds, which means there are no commissions charged for these purchases. Look for "No-Load" funds that have an investment objective and performance record that fits your purpose for buying the fund.

Index Funds

An index fund is a type of mutual fund whose objective is to perform in a way that tracks a particular investment sector of the market. One of the biggest advantages an index fund has over other mutual funds is its significantly lower management cost than other mutual funds—and the longer a fund is held the more important those costs can become. According to Warren Buffet, one of the nation's most successful investors, "For an individual investor an index fund is the best individual fund." This statement is coming from one of the most respected investors in the world, who has consistently beaten the market for more than 50 years.

Historically, the Standard & Poor 500 (S&P 500) has returned 10.8%, disregarding inflation, since its inception in 1957. **However, it's important to note that investment markets are volatile and have experienced many years where there have been dramatic losses.** For example, if you invested in the Vanguard S&P 500 Index Mutual Fund in January of 2000, you would have had an average annual return of less than 1% per year as of 31 December 2011 (although there were years of substantial gains and years of substantial losses during that 12 year period).

Considerations Before You Invest

• What is the historical growth?
• Is the company management stable?
• How risky is the investment?

Target Date Mutual Funds

These funds are similar to the new "L"-Lifestyle Funds available in your TSP. Many mutual fund companies, banks and insurance companies have Target Date Funds available with target dates into the future. You could select a "target" date that you might retire or perhaps a date that you want to have available for your child's college education. Like the "L" fund, these Target Date Funds hold a mix of assets that are adjusted by the mutual fund manager so the portfolio becomes more conservative as the fund reaches maturity.

Dollar Cost Averaging

This strategy involves making consistent investments into your fund, regardless of its day-to-day performance. This is the easiest way to compensate for the market's inevitable ups and downs, because you can buy pieces of your portfolio when it is high, as well as when it is low, with the idea that over time you are getting an "average" price for your portfolio. Investing in the TSP each paycheck is an example of dollar cost averaging. You can do the same thing by having a specified amount automatically transferred from your checking account to an investment of your choosing in your Roth IRA or your Traditional IRA each month or week.

Dollar Cost Averaging Put $50 in your mutual fund on a set day of every month regardless of market prices.

Final Note

Don't invest into any particular financial vehicle until you do research online or at the library and with multiple professionals prior to making a decision. Many professionals are willing to discuss your options and help educate you—without you investing money. Making the correct investment choices will make a substantial difference when you reach your financial freedom. Reference this website, *www.investor.gov*, for more insight on different investment vehicles.

Education is a lifelong process that benefits individuals and entire communities and countries and helps lay the foundation of the future.

Ronald Reagan
United States President

Education

BLUF:
The world is becoming faster, smarter and more digital. It is a Soldier's responsibility to stay competitive and sharp. College and graduate school education is the approved solution.

Discussion:
Education extends beyond a Soldier's experience in the Army. This section will discuss:
• Why college matters (FACTS)
• How to plan for it and pay for it
• Dependent's education benefits
• Post 9-11 GI Bill explained

Why College Matters!
For Soldiers on active duty there are numerous benefits to earning a college degree.
1. It directly affects promotion points. An E-4 can earn up to 75 promotion points (out of 800) for a civilian education. As an E-5, you can earn up to 100 points (of 800 total) for a civilian education. This trend shows that as you gain rank the emphasis on college-level education becomes greater.
2. Education will NEVER be more affordable. **www.GoArmyEd.com** makes earning a college degree virtually free for those seeking an undergraduate degree and significantly reduces the cost of graduate degrees.
3. At the point of transition, out of active duty service, a Soldier retains the Post 9-11 GI Bill benefits for dependents. Two college degrees for the price of one!

Veterans
Even though veterans who have transitioned out of service are still eligible for benefits through the Post 9-11 GI Bill, many veterans let these benefits go unused. Although your personal circumstances will contribute greatly to your decisions, there is a significant long-term advantage to earning your

college or professional degree with help from your Post 9-11 GI Bill benefits.

1. **Earnings**—Generally speaking a person's average earnings nearly double with a bachelor's degree over a high school diploma ($27,915 to $51,206) and, on average, individuals with a graduate degree annually earn $74,602.

2. **Costs**—Even with only partial benefits, working towards a college degree can be affordable.

3. **Unemployment**—According to the January 2012 jobs report, the unemployment rate among those with a college degree is approximately 4% while the unemployment rate of those with a high school degree is around 10%.

Most everyone desires a comfortable lifestyle, and a correlation can be drawn between a person's level of education, and their respective personal finances. In general, the formula is simple: more education = more money. College debt can put a burden on your financial life, but the military has a number of programs that enables ANYONE to invest in education at an extremely low/no cost to the individual.

How to Attend?

There are numerous ways in which a Soldier can earn his or her college degree. The first thing to understand is that a college degree is awarded based upon the completion of a certain number of credits in specific courses. It is important to understand that college credits can be earned in and out of the classroom.

Online College Classes

Distance Learning

This is the method by which most active duty Soldiers pursue their college degree. Schedule an appointment with the local Army Education Center to establish a college enrollment plan and speak with a counselor one-on-one about your specific circumstances. Additional information can be found at **www.GoArmyEd.com**.

Outside the Classroom

College Level Examination Program (CLEP)
CLEP is the most widely accepted credit-by-examination program in the U.S. and the Army offers these courses at no cost to the Soldier. CLEP exams allow you to demonstrate to a college that you have mastered the material and that you do not need to take the course. With CLEP tests, Soldiers can save time and money by earning between three and 12 college credits for each CLEP test taken.

The Army provides free CLEP test preparation through Army Knowledge Online (AKO). Go to **www.us.army.mil** → self service → my library → practice test, careers, and resumes or college search. This will provide you with access to many career and educational planning tools. In addition to CLEP prep, any of the same locations offer access to Armed Services Vocational Aptitude Battery (ASVAB) prep and resume building tools.

College Credit for Army Course Work
The Army and the American Council on Education Registry Transcript System (AARTS) have certified certain military courses that translate into college credit. This saves the Army time and money and reduces the amount of time you have to spend in the classroom. An AARTS transcript is electronically sent directly to the college or institution of higher learning of your choosing. A list of eligible Army courses is available at **www.acenet.edu**.

There are certain Army courses than can translate into college credit.

How to Pay for It?
GoArmyEd is used by Active Army, National Guard, and Army Reserve Soldiers, as a one-stop shop to request Army Tuition Assistance (TA), and manage college education. GoArmyEd partners with 25 fully accredited colleges, and offers more than 140 certificates and degree programs, provided 100% online. The biggest advantage of the GoArmyEd system is the money that is made available. **Every student has an annual ceiling of $4,500 with a per semester hour cap of $250 that doesn't have to be repaid.** This is typically more than enough to cover the educational costs of most schools enrolled in the program.

For enlisted Soldiers there is no additional service obligation for participating in this program. Officers must serve an additional two years (incurred at course enrollment) upon course completion.

For more information on GoArmyEd, the best place to start is to visit your nearest Army Education Center (AEC). A list of education centers can be found at **www.goarmyed.com**. Go to the AEC and sit down with a counselor to develop your roadmap to earning a college degree.

Post 9-11 GI Bill

In 2011-2012 the average cost of a full time student in a four-year public university program was $12,316. By the completion of your four-year degree, you will owe or have paid more than $50,000, and, as previously stated, this is a worthwhile cost because of your future earning potential. This is where Soldiers have a huge advantage. **Soldiers that have (1) served 90 days or more of continuous active duty service or (2) served 30 days and were medically discharged from the military after 9-11 are eligible for the benefits of the post 9-11 GI Bill.**

Post 9-11 GI Bill Benefits Chart

Service	Benefits
36 Cumulative Months	100%
30 Cumulative Months	90%
24 Cumulative Months	80%
18 Cumulative Months	70%
12 Cumulative Months	60%
6 Cumulative Months	50%
90 Cumulative Days	40%

The Post 9-11 GI Bill was created to cover the cost of education for our nation's veterans. The current GI Bill is marked by upfront tuition payments, a housing allowance (BAH rate is at the E-5 with dependents level), and a book stipend. It seems complex, but the concept is very simple: **unless you were medically separated, you get the maximum of the post 9-11 GI bill after being on active duty for three years.**

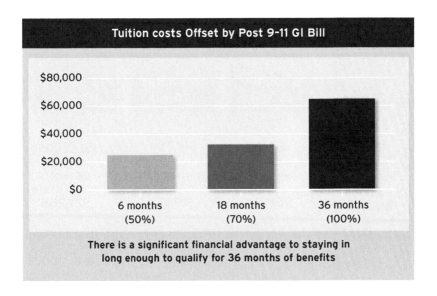

Tuition costs Offset by Post 9-11 GI Bill

There is a significant financial advantage to staying in
long enough to qualify for 36 months of benefits

Yellow Ribbon Program (YRP)
Many private schools, with tuition and costs exceeding the Post 9-11 benefits, participate in the YRP. The YRP is a Veterans Affairs program that doubles the value of your GI benefits. **To be eligible for the YRP, a Soldier must qualify for 100% of the GI Bill benefits.** To determine if your intended school participates in the YRP check with the VA department at **www.gibill.va.gov/GI_Bill**.

The graph above demonstrates a 200% increase in the amount of funding received by staying in for 36 months in comparison to departing after 18 months.

After Undergraduate Study
For those who already possess an undergraduate degree, the Post 9-11 GI Bill still presents an incredible opportunity to further your education. Regardless of the degree type, the rules above apply.

Time Served	6 months (50%)	18 months (70 %)	36 months (100%)
Tuition	$8,750	$12,250	$17,500 + ($17,500- YRP)
Living Allowance (varies by zip code)	$13,644	$19,104	$27,288
Books	$500	$700	$1,000
Total GI Bill Benefits	$22,894	$32,054	$63,288

Annual Benefits Timeline

Dependent Education
Regardless of the educational benefits available to your spouse and your children, the approved solution to fund their continued education is two-fold: develop a sound savings and investment strategy and know the rules of Army financial aid programs.

How Much Does College Cost?
Like any military exercise you must know your end state before you can begin executing your mission. Similarly, before you can begin developing your personal college savings strategy it is critical to know how much you really need to save. Let's start with how much college costs using the figures provided by **www.collegeboard.com**.

Quickly you can see that the yearly tuition price of a collegiate education varies from $2,963 at a two-year college to $36,000 at a private four-year school. This demonstrates that your spouse or children's educational aspirations can greatly impact the amount of money that you need to save. The best resource to determine which college option is the best for your dependents is the Army Education Center (AEC). AEC has assigned counselors available for individual educational consultations. They will steer you in the right direction so that you only pay for the educational level needed.

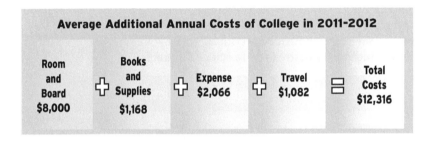

Average Additional Annual Costs of College in 2011-2012

Room and Board $8,000 + Books and Supplies $1,168 + Expense $2,066 + Travel $1,082 = Total Costs $12,316

How Much Will It Actually Cost You?

There is a real difference between what the cost of tuition is and what the end-of-the-year bill will show. Some other additional billable costs to take into consideration are: room and board, books and supplies, travel, as well as funds for personal expense items like a cell phone, field trips, pizza, etc.

How to Pay

The best way to help pay this bill is to develop an echeloned savings strategy. This four-tiered strategy consists of:
1. Cost cutting (budgeting)
2. Scholarship
3. Financial aid
4. Developing a savings and investment plan

Budget

We all know how to cut costs, but very few of us do it well. Generally, this concept is simple: if you don't need it, don't buy it. Cost cutting rests on your ability to plan your purchasing and have the discipline not to "impulse buy." If saving for a big purchase like college, refer to the Savings chapter for more advice on saving.

Savings Plan

Any financial planner worth his salt will tell you the single most important factor in an investment portfolio is time. The amount of time you have before you need to withdraw money will greatly impact the method and strategy you use to reach your goal. For this reason, executing your college savings plan EARLY is critical. When your child is born or your spouse indicates a desire to go to school, immediately begin to save.

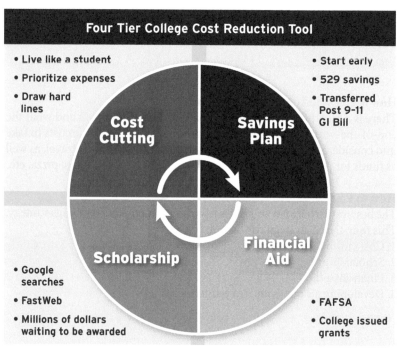

Four Tier College Cost Reduction Tool

- Live like a student
- Prioritize expenses
- Draw hard lines

Cost Cutting

Savings Plan

- Start early
- 529 savings
- Transferred Post 9-11 GI Bill

- Google searches
- FastWeb
- Millions of dollars waiting to be awarded

Scholarship

Financial Aid

- FAFSA
- College issued grants

28% of full-time private four-year college students are at schools charging $36,000 or more yearly in tuition and fees.

Savings Plan Options

Saving for a college education is no longer limited to cash in a shoebox or a vintage baseball card collection. There are many savings options for a Soldier. Below are some of the more prominent types:

(1) US Savings Bonds Series EE Savings Bond
- Guaranteed to double in value 20 years after purchase
- Applied toward tuition and fees, not room and board
- Tax advantage for married couples making less than $91,750 annual taxable income
- Purchased directly from **www.treasurydirect.gov**

(2) Coverdell Education Savings Account
- Save for tuition expenses and write-off your savings as a deduction on your taxes
- Can be rolled from one child to another
- $2,000 per child per year

(3) State Sponsored Qualified Tuition Plans (529 Plans)
- Two types: prepaid programs and savings programs
- High maximum contribution limits are allowed—sometimes up to $375,000 per beneficiary
- State taxes are waived in some states for residents; deductions on contributions are allowed in others
- Contributions are considered completed gifts and are excluded from estates, which makes the plans attractive to grandparents, who can change the beneficiaries to other grandchildren as funds are needed
- Information can be found **www.collegesavings.org** and **www.savingforcollege.com**

Financial Aid

Financial aid makes up the difference between what college costs and what you can afford. The majority, even those with a disciplined cost-cutting strategy and a sound college savings plan, will not be able to cover the full cost of our dependent's college education. Fortunately, this is not a condition unique to Soldiers. People all across the country find college expenses more than their salary and savings can absorb. This reality has led the federal government, state governments, and colleges across the country to adopt financial aid programs.

If you are about to finance a dependent's college education, what determines how much you can afford? The answer is driven by your Free Application for Federal Student Aid (FAFSA). The output of the FAFSA is commonly referred to as your dependent's Expected Family Contribution (EFC). This EFC determines the amount the government and college expects you to contribute to your dependent's education. To find your EFC utilize the calculator found at **www.apps.collegeboard.org.**

Anything you manage to save for college will increase the amount that YOU are expected to contribute (your EFC) by 5.5% if saving are in your name, and 24% if savings are in your child's name. In other words, every $100,000 you save in your name for college will increase your EFC by almost $22,000 over four years. If the same $100,000 was held in your child's name then your EFC will be dramatically higher. You will be heavily penalized for having money in your child's name rather than your own name when it comes to applying for financial aid.

> If your child's **Expected Family Contribution** is determined to be $10,000 and her college's total cost is $15,000 then your child would be eligible for $5,000 in financial aid. If the total college cost was $50,000 then your child would be eligible for $40,000 in aid. Regardless of the college cost, your expected contribution is the same.

There are four main categories of financial aid:

1. **Grants**— Grants do not require repayment; however, grants are issued to students in packages to alleviate the immediate financial stress associated with getting educated.

**Grant —
no obligation
to repay**

**Loan —
must be repaid.**

2. **Loans**—Loans must be repaid, but come in two main categories:
   - Subsidized—awarded on the basis of financial need. While you are a student, you will not be charged any interest before you begin repaying the loan because the federal government subsidizes the interest during this time.
   - Unsubsidized—interest is payable from the time the money is first disbursed until it is repaid in full—even while you are a student. The interest is capitalized, meaning that you pay interest on any interest that has already accrued.
3. **Scholarship**—One way to bridge the gap between what you can afford (your EFC) and what you need (the school's total bill) is a scholarship. These are are privately funded grants that students apply for and compete against other students. The scope and nature of scholarships varies greatly; however, there are millions of dollars available. The key to finding the right scholarship is to START EARLY and RESEARCH. Utilize scholarship search engines like FastWeb and SallieMae.
4. **Post 9-11 GI Bill**—The Post 9-11 GI Bill is a legitimate option for dependents to significantly reduce your out-of-pocket college expenses. Soldiers can transfer benefits totaling up to 36 months.

To transfer benefits to dependents

1. Insure all dependents are registered through DEERS
2. Go to: **www.dmdc.osd.mil**
3. Sign in and fill out the milConnect portal application at **www.milconnect.dmdc.mil**
4. Once your transfer request is approved, apply for your dependents' certificate of eligibility at **www.ebenefits.va.gov**. Any questions call the Department of Veterans affairs at 1-888-GIBILL1
5. After receiving certificates, dependents should present these to the school or program of choice.

GI Bill Transfer Requirements

Soldier Eligibility
Six years of service (active or selective reserve) with additional commitment of four years

Dependent Eligibility
Soldier's Spouse
- Divorce will not affect eligibility–Soldier has option to revoke
- May use benefits while Soldier on active duty
- Can be used 15 years after Soldier separates from active duty

Soldier's Child (benefits can be split)
- A child's marriage will not affect eligibility
- Cannot use after 26 years old
- Must have high school degree or turn age 17

Scholarships for Military Children

The Scholarship for Military Children Program was created in recognition of the contributions of military families to the readiness of the fighting force. These scholarships are organized and distributed by the Defense Commissary Agency and the Fisher House Foundation. A minimum of one $1500 scholarship will be awarded at every commissary location where qualified applications are received. To date the scholarship has awarded nearly $9 million. Find more information at **www.militaryscholar.org.**

Standardized Test Prep

SAT/ACT

Every Soldier is entitled to several SAT and ACT college test programs. A general rule is that a high SAT/ACT score sometimes leads to some type of college scholarship.

- **www.march2success.com** is a free, no obligation, online test prep tool to help anyone improve their test scores. It provides study aids and practice tests.
- eKnowledge provides all Soldiers with a free DVD on SAT/ACT prep through SAT/ACT PowerPrep. Visit **www.eknowledge.com** for more information and to request DVDs mailed to your home.
- Free SAT prep through the DoD Military Library website at **www.nelnetsolutions.com.**

Borrowing Money

Even with effective saving, cost-cutting and financial aid you or your child may have to borrow money to fully cover educational costs. Most educational loans are applied for through the college's financial aid office. Below are typical loan options.

Loan	Need Based & Subsidized	Borrower	Interest Rate	Description
Types of Student Loans				
Perkins	Yes	Student	5% (fixed)	Students with the highest need; $5,500 per year
Subsidized Stafford	Yes	Student	3.4% (fixed)	Gov't pays interest while student in school; max $3,500 per year
Unsubsidized Stafford	No	Student	6.8% (fixed)	Used to pay EFC; amount subtracted out of subsidized loan
Parent PLUS	No	Parent	7.9% (fixed)	Parents borrow up to total cost minus student aid received
Private/ State	No	Student	Varies, but high	Do your research

Note–Subsidized means that you (the borrower) do not pay interest on the loan until you are finished with school.

Final Note

Education is critical. Soldiers and their families are eligible for many free or reduced cost mechanisms to become educated. Again, do your research and take advantage of what's being offered.

*Fun is like life insurance;
the older you get,
the more it costs.*

Kin Hubbard
American Cartoonist

Insurance

BLUF:

Insurance is used to protect you, your family, your dependents, and your assets in the case of unforeseen events. Think of the right kind of insurance as serving as the body armor and eye protection for your financial security. We say the "right kind" of insurance because just as with so many things, there are shoddy insurance companies and insurance products, and dishonest sales people who have their own interest at heart, not yours.

Discussion:

Insurance is an extremely complex area and we will only scratch the surface. We will, however, lay out the basics and suggest some questions to ask and resources to reach out to that we believe will help you better understand the insurance industry.

Life Insurance: Different Types

a. Servicemembers' Group Life Insurance (SGLI)
b. Term Insurance
c. Whole Life Insurance
d. Universal Life Insurance

The first analysis is determining what your financial obligations are, and planning accordingly. Financial obligations include things like burial costs, outstanding debts, and income that your family will require for future planned expenses.

In the next section we address the fact that maximum SGLI coverage is $400,000. Although that is a lot of money, if you're the primary breadwinner in a family, it's not nearly enough to take care of your spouse and children for the long term if something happens to you. One way to look at this is to consider that your survivors could draw about 4% per year from the $400,000 in hopes that the principal would be able to keep pace with inflation over the years: that's $16,000 a year. Now consider how far that amount would go in meeting your family's financial needs. Of course they could draw more each year, but then it becomes more likely that the money will run out much sooner.

Life Insurance

Service members Group Life Insurance (SGLI) is a VA program that provides low-cost group life insurance to members of the uniformed services. Members are automatically insured under SGLI for the maximum amount of $400,000 unless an election is filed reducing the insurance in $50,000 increments. Visit **www.va.gov** for more information.

Facts:

1. Cost—$3.25 for each $50,000 increment or $28 per month for full SGLI coverage
2. Family—SGLI automatically provides $100,000 for the spouse and $10,000 for each child
3. Taxes—Exempt from income taxation
4. Beneficiary—It is your choice who receives your SGLI death benefit; however if you are married, the government says you must notify your spouse if he/she is not the primary beneficiary
5. $400,000 and a $100,000 Service Death Gratuity; active-duty service members can have $500,000 of coverage
6. SGLI provides free coverage for 120 days after you leave active duty
7. You have the opportunity to convert to Veterans Group Life Insurance (VGLI). These premiums are very expensive and increase every five years.
8. There is no extension to your $100,000 Service Death Gratuity once you get out of the military
9. Theoretically you lose a $500,000 policy when you leave the military.

Term Insurance

Term Insurance, sometimes called "pure insurance," is life insurance that is in place for a term of years, normally building up no cash value and expiring without value at the end of the agreed-upon term. Because this kind of insurance is relatively inexpensive, you can purchase more coverage at a lower cost than most other kinds of life insurance. You can purchase policies for different terms to cover you for periods or for specific purposes when your death would have the most financial impact on your family—such as when your kids are young and still living at home or to make sure there would be money for college. Typical term periods are 10, 15, 20, 25 and 30 years. This is the type of insurance that SGLI provides. It goes away as soon as you get out of the military, regardless of how much money you have contributed throughout the years.

SGLI members are automatically insured for $400,000.

Whole Life Insurance

Whole Life Insurance offers protection for the whole of life, proceeds being payable at death. Premiums may be paid under a continuous premium arrangement or on a limited payment basis for virtually any desired period of years.

Universal Life Insurance

With Universal Life Insurance, the insurance company assumes an interest rate and the cost of insurance, and projects a premium. If the insurance companies' projections do not come through, then you may have to come up with higher premiums later to keep the policy in force or have lower than expected cash values, or even lose the policy.

Auto Insurance

Be sure that you understand each part of your coverage. Ask yourself and your insurance provider a couple of basic questions:

- What is your deductible and what does a deductible mean to your insurance company?
- How does your policy protect you from various claims?
- Is the coverage that you currently have enough to protect you, your family and your assets?
- In the event of an accident what happens to you and those in your car if you or your passengers are seriously injured?
- What is the process of making a claim?

Renter's Insurance

Often there is a limit on the amount of coverage for certain items like jewelry, guns, electronics, collections, antiques and other high dollar items. Have a conversation with your provider and ask:

- What is covered under this policy and for how much?

The USAA Educational Foundation is an excellent resource for information on all insurance-related matters.

• How will your policy protect you from claims if someone is injured while in your rental unit?
• Is all of your personal property protected for its "replacement value" rather than its depreciated value?

Homeowner's Insurance

You'd have the same questions for your agent as with renter's insurance. Also ask:

• What you would receive if your dwelling were partially or totally destroyed?
• What would the insurance company pay in order for you to "replace" your home or the part of your home that was damaged or destroyed?

Personal Property Coverage

Insurance companies have different names for this coverage but it has to do with items that may not be completely covered under your Renter's or Homeowner's policy; items mentioned above that might have their own limits of coverage such as jewelry, guns, electronics, collections, antiques, etc. This type of insurance comes with an additional cost. Ask your agent:

• What degree are these items covered under my regular policy?
• How much will it cost to insure your high value items for their full replacement value?

Ratings of Insurance Companies

AM Best, Moody's, and Standard and Poor's are several of the rating services that evaluate the financial strength of insurance companies. You are relying on the financial strength of the insurance company you deal with to have the financial resources to pay your claim if and when you need them to follow through on the provisions of your policy. Additionally, Consumer Reports magazine rates insurance companies in a number of different categories; most libraries carry copies you can review. The USAA Educational Foundation is an excellent resource for information on all insurance-related matters.

Final Note

There is a type of insurance for virtually everything. When selecting your coverage and provider, understand what you are getting for your money by doing a little research and shopping around.

Do not follow where the path may lead. Go instead where there is no path and leave a trail.

Ralph Waldo Emerson
American Author

Temporary Duty

BLUF:

Traveling on Temporary Duty (TDY) is something that virtually every Soldier will do at least once during his or her career. Whether you are traveling to a military school or as part of your assignment's official capacity, knowing what to do and what not to do can save a great deal of time, frustration and money.

- Five steps to TDY travel
- Reimbursable expenses
- TDY resources

Discussion:

TDY is the means by which Soldiers travel on official business. Since TDY is considered business, your work-related expenses are going to be paid. The main expense is lodging, but there are a host of other expenses that are reimbursable when you are traveling on official TDY. Expenses are paid when you return from your official travel, and file your TDY paperwork, so Soldiers who travel frequently are encouraged to sign up for a government credit card. A government travel card will allow for the payment of the expenses of your TDY trip without using your personal credit cards.

In addition to these expenses, you will receive the Meals and Incidental Expenses (M&IE) rate for the location of your travel. This rate varies by location, but it is a generous amount and will cover breakfast, lunch and dinner. Unlike lodging, M&IE will come to you as the traveler, regardless of how much money you spent. Visit **www.defensetravel.ots.mil** to find out what the M&IE rate is for your TDY location.

Reimbursable Expenses

- Passport and visa fees
- Costs of transportation to and from the terminal
- Parking fees at the terminal
- Mileage to and from the terminal
- Airport taxes
- Transportation costs at TDY location
- Baggage tips
- Lodging taxes
- Resort fees
- Late checkout fees
- Office rooms used for official business
- Storage rooms for official business
- Calls home
- Laundry / dry cleaning / clothes press (seven night military–$2/day limit)

In order to initiate a TDY you will input your travel reservation into the Defense Travel System (DTS); think of DTS as your online travel agent service. Through DTS you can reserve car rentals, hotels, flights, input anticipated expenses, and see your M&IE rate. The Army fully embraces DTS and all travel in the foreseeable future will utilize this system. Your unit will have a DTS manager, and he or she will serve as the Point of Contact (POC) for all DTS-related questions and issues, as well as providing instructions on your unit's SOP for reserving travel through this system.

Five Steps—Smart TDY Travel

Now that the general facts are on the table, let's discuss how you can maximize your official travel.

1. **Talk to your unit's DTS POC.** Find out how to use the system properly. Your DTS rep will be able to assist you by explaining some of the specifics particular to your unit. Plan and input TDY into DTS early. Learn more about DTS at **www.defensetravel.osd.mil**

2. **Don't spend all of your M&IE.** Although saving $20 on meals is not going to make you rich, you are bound to spend money on items that are not considered reimbursable expenses.

3. **Get a travel rewards card.** According to Chapter 301 of GSA Federal Travel Regulations, the head of your agency (commander of your unit) or his/her designee has the authority to let you use a personal credit card for certain aspects of your officially sponsored government travel. With this exemption you are allowed to use a personal travel card and receive the benefits of using the card. You will be reimbursed for all official TDY-related expenses: hotel, rental car and airline points/miles points are yours to keep. If your credit is good enough to secure a travel credit card, you should get one and use it for the hotel and rental car, and pay it off immediately upon your return when you receive your reimbursement. Any promotional benefits or materials received from a travel service provider in connection with official travel may be retained for personal use, if such items are obtained under the same conditions as those offered to the general public and at no additional cost to the government.

4. **Pay off everything**—to include government credit card—at the end of every trip. Not paying off your credit card will lead to interest penalties

and can potentially negatively affect your credit. Your government travel card is ultimately your responsibility.

5. **Save all of your receipts!** If you do not have receipts you will not have the proof needed to be reimbursed for your expenses. Rental car, fuel, parking, hotel, and other expenses need to be included in your voucher as substantiating documents. It is much more difficult to substantiate these expenses without receipts.

FINAL NOTE

TDY is an awesome opportunity. Take advantage when the government sends you around the world by sticking to a budget and properly claiming your expenses.

*Whatever
your life's work is,
do it well.*

*Martin Luther King Jr.
Noble Peace Prize Winner*

Permanent Change of Station

BLUF:
A Permanent Change of Station (PCS) move is something that every military member will go through many times throughout a military career. Knowing the process will make this critical part of your career easier.

Discussion:
There are three main options when you PCS: (1) Do it yourself (DITY) (2) Partial DITY (3) Household goods (HHG).
- Pros and cons of PCS move options
- DITY move checklist
- PCS resources

Military Moves			
	DITY	**Household Goods**	**Partial**
PROS	• Largest opportunity to make more money • Most control	• Easiest; least hassle	• Incorporate pros from HHG and DITY
CONS	• Lots of work and time • Strong plan needed to be successful	• You won't be able to make any money • Higher risk for damage	• Incorporate cons from HHG and DITY
OVERALL	• Best suited for young, single service members	• Best suited for those with large families and tight time restraints	• Perfect if you can manage to pack on your own

Full DITY
A full DITY is the Soldier's alternative to using a military contracted moving company: reimbursement is based on the weight of the items and the distance to your new duty station. Contact your Household Goods Station.

Pre-Move Full DITY Checklist

Ideal situation is to find a place to live at your new duty station before you get there.

- ✔ PCS orders (five copies)
- ✔ Directions and addresses
- ✔ Temporary housing
- ✔ Rest stops along route
- ✔ Weigh stations (must be military approved CAT certified)
- ✔ POV inspection before traveling
- ✔ Post office and complete your change of address form.
- ✔ Make contact with businesses that provide services (i.e. phone, cable, utility, etc) and provide a termination date to these companies for their service
- ✔ Notify the companies of your new address so they can forward the last bill to your new mailing address
- ✔ Privately owned vehicle (POV) or rental truck (if you have a rental truck make sure you keep the rental paperwork and receipt)
- ✔ Application for DITY Move and Counseling Checklist (DD Form 2278)
- ✔ Certified empty weight ticket for each vehicle with name, your Social Security number and signature of weight master
- ✔ Certified loaded weight ticket for each vehicle with name, your Social Security number and signature of weight master
- ✔ Copy of vehicle title or registration
- ✔ Weigh your vehicle empty with a full tank of gas and no driver when on the scale. **Reminder: you are only allowed to use certified scales.** Most large military installations have certified weigh stations within a 15 mile radius

Through this program the Soldier can receive up to 100% of the Government Constructive Cost (GCC) of the move. The GCC is the amount that the government would have paid a contractor to move the Soldier—limited to the Soldier's maximum allowed household goods weight. In exchange for the Soldier receiving this payment, the service member must pack, load, and unload all of his or her property or contract it out to someone else. Prior to conducting a DITY move, ensure that you have all of the required paperwork in order to receive your full reimbursement. **Soldiers are authorized a money advance to help defray the associated moving costs.**

To make the full DITY move worthwhile, you should be honest with yourself: the larger your family, the less likely you should opt for a full DITY move. **If you are a single Soldier, without a great deal of personal goods, a full DITY will be more beneficial.**

Handling the DITY Process

- Contact your local Transportation Office
- Decide on a strategy for your DITY move
- Choose from the options available for DITY move
- Rental truck (note not reimbursable)
- Ala carte moving service (www.ditymovers.com)
- Pack your belongings
- Load your belongings into the truck/trailer
- Travel to new location
- Unload your belongings
- File for reimbursement

Tax Implications

All payments associated with your DITY move are considered income, and as income it can be taxed. As a result, it is important to document your trip expenses such as gas and tolls in order to reduce the tax withholdings (deductions). Also, you receive per-diem during your PCS move and therefore cannot claim meals or hotel expenses.

DITY Tax Implications Example:

- SFC Smith moves his own goods. The weight of the goods and the distance moved work out to be a $5,000 reimbursement from the Army.
- SFC Smith submits receipts for expenses amounting to $3,000.
- The difference between the two amounts ($2,000) is the amount that is subject to federal tax: 28% of the $2,000 ($560) is kept by the government as withholding.
- The payment to SFC Smith will be equal to the total reimbursement ($5,000) minus the government withholding ($560).
- Bottom Line: SFC Smith gets $4,440.

Movement

Receive and hold onto your second weight ticket from the weight master for your travel claim. If for whatever reason, you cannot weigh your vehicle locally, there will be plenty of weigh stations designed for truckers where you can weigh your vehicle along the highways.

Within 45 days of arrival at your receiving unit, you must process your full DITY move through your Transportation Office at your new duty station. **By the end of the trip, you should have the following items in your possession:**

- One copy of your PCS orders
- Original DD Form 2278 (DITY application)
- Empty weight ticket
- Loaded weight ticket
- DD Form 1351-2 (Travel Voucher or Sub-voucher)
- Receipts for fuel and tolls
- Copy of power of attorney (POA) if needed
- Copy of vehicle title or registration
- Four copies of your leave form

Advantages:

- Control over possessions. When you arrive at your new duty station, your possessions arrive.
- Typically, will make money from this move. The more weight that you have and the longer the distance that you travel, the more money the government will pay for you to move yourself.

Disadvantages:

- No insurance on HHG. You break it, you buy it.
- Lots of work and time.

Partial DITY

You can make a little money and have fewer headaches—an advantage over full DITY.

1. The US government will pay to ship two vehicles if you are married and one vehicle if you are single.
2. The partial DITY allows a family to box up the majority of their HHG that would not fit in the family vehicle and use that vehicle to transport the family and personal property. Go through the house and put all of the items that you are taking with you in a separate location, i.e. the garage, empty closet, or extra bathroom. Let the packers know not to pack these specific items.

- **Hint:** Place like items together so the packers know to pack these items together and when it comes time to unpack, you will find yourself much better organized and more efficient.

Advance Payment

While filling your initial DITY move paperwork, the Travel Office is going to ask if you want to take an advance on your DITY move; essentially asking if you want a portion of your money upfront in order to help with the cost of your move.

- ***Note:*** *Weight Estimate: If your advance from your partial DITY exceeds the actual amount owed to you by the government (certified by final weigh ticket), you will have to pay the difference back.*

HHG Government Contracted

This method involves allowing the government to move your HHG, either through **www.move.mil** or through your Transportation Office, in order to process the paperwork for the HHG shipment.

One of the great things about HHG is that you are insured for all items annotated on your moving list. **In essence anything that is damaged will be covered by the government.**

Behind the scenes: a company will be designated to pack your HHG and load everything onto their truck. Be sure to ask your Transportation Office for a complete list of restricted packing material for the HHGs. There are certain items that you are not allowed to move, i.e. propane tanks. Military rank and number of dependents are two things that determine the weight limit on household items.

Helpful Hints

• Take pictures or video record all of your possessions prior to moving.
• Take your complete dress uniform with you and at least one complete duty uniform. The bottom line is that things tend to get lost or misplaced during these moves. Think and plan for things to be lost during the process. If there is something that you cannot live without (for example, your uniform) then you should pack it with you.
• *Note: It can take months to receive reimbursement for lost items or for the warehouse to find your items.*

Family

It is important that once a Soldier receives his official orders, NOT a Request for Orders (RFO), that he notifies his or her spouse that the move is official.

• Spouses will notify their employers of the upcoming move. **The spouse should not quit a job until the military member has received official orders.**

Children

1. Obtain your children's school records before you depart to the new duty station. Each school is different but the school's main office should be able to assist with the process.
2. Once you arrive at the new duty station, you will need to enroll your child in school.
3. The new school will ask for your child's records before enrolling anyone. Provide your children's official school records and any additional information from their old school.
4. Make sure you obtain copies of your family members' medical records. You can obtain these records from the primary care manager (PCM), dentist and any specialists or other medical personnel your family has visited while at your last duty station. Conduct a final check before departure that ensures that your pet is up-to-date with all vaccinations. In case you are flying to your new duty station, obtain a few copies of the vaccination records.

Final Note

Moving can be incredibly stressful, but the military has done a great job at making it less stressful. The on-post services dedicated to moving you exist to serve you. Go into their office and have them explain the process so you are best prepared to negotiate the challenges.

Life's a voyage that's homeward bound.

Herman Melville
Author

Housing

BLUF:
There is no single right answer to the question of whether it is better for Soldiers to buy or rent. Each Soldier has a unique personal circumstance that weighs heavily in the ultimate housing decision he or she makes. This chapter serves to present facts and help you to make an informed decision.

Discussion:
One of the single most important financial decisions that you will make as a Soldier is whether you will rent or purchase a home. It is important because it is one of the largest purchases—potentially—that anyone can make. There are significant benefits to both renting and buying, and each needs to be carefully researched and considered. This chapter covers the benefits and potential drawbacks of on-post vs. off-post living, as well as renting vs. buying.
• On-post vs. off-post
• Rent vs. buy
• VA loan explained
• Benefits of Army home ownership

On-Post vs. Off-Post
The first thing to understand when approaching the question of on- or off-post living is that both types of living vary based on the location duty station. Generally speaking, if you are PCS'ing to the Pentagon, your off-post options are virtually endless. If you are PCS'ing to Korea you have little to no off-post housing and must live on-base—and then there is everything in between.

There are, however, a couple of commonalities that can get you started. Almost every post has a housing office and a series of off-post residential experts, which can be easily found via the Internet. There are also some general considerations about on-post living that will help you evaluate the options.

On-Post Advantages	On-Post Disadvantages
• Proximity to services	• Your entire BAH is used for the housing (plus utility costs on some bases)
• Child care / schooling	
• PX / commissary	• Largely segregated from off-base community
• Community	
• Reduced daily commute	• Must abide by post regulations
• Security—especially during deployments	• Pets limitations
	• Sometimes long wait for ideal housing
• Avoid predatory lending / renting	
• No hassle PCS	• Lack of housing options

Moving on-post is a personal decision that fits the needs of many Soldiers. To fully evaluate the on-post conditions contact your future duty station's housing office and use the chart above to guide your talking points. Your future duty station's housing office can be located and contacted at **https://www.housing.army.mil/ah/**. This site will also provide you with detailed reference information, post policies, BAH rates, school information, maps and more.

Renting vs. Buying

Soldiers who choose to reside off-post have a lot of decisions to make and hurdles to avoid. The next few sections will focus on this critically important decision.

Take the decision to live off-post very seriously. If this decision is miscalculated, your finances, quality of life, and ability to perform as a Soldier can be severely affected. Be honest with yourself and sit down with your spouse to think about the following considerations:

Considerations

- **Length of PCS orders:** The shorter the orders the less incentive to buy.

- **Retirement location:** Could you see yourself living in this location after retirement?

- **Strength of local economy:** Is your home going to hold value, and will people want to rent it?

- **Interest rates:** Use your VA loan to lock in attractive rates with a small down payment.

- **Family needs:** How many dependents do you have, how close do they have to be to post?

- **Personal finance:** Which option best aligns with your personal finance strategy?

- **Unit deployment schedule:** Can you be a landlord while deployed?

- **Reselling:** Ask your realtor how difficult it will be to sell in a few years. A good realtor knows what areas are selling more houses than others.

If, after thinking about these considerations, you still are not certain, you should seek the advice of your chain of command or a personal financial planner to fully evaluate all of your needs. For those of you who have decided to pursue off-post living, the remainder of this chapter is dedicated to helping you make an informed and well prepared decision, and ensuring that you know which questions to ask, and to whom to direct your inquiries.

Renting

The best place to start the hunt for a rental unit is to contact the post's housing office. See if they have any recommended realtors who have a good record of dealings with Soldiers. Contact these listing agents and get a list of available units that fit your specifications. Most posts will require that the rental unit gain approval from the housing office prior to occupancy.

Do your research. Searching for off-post housing on one of the major Internet search engines will yield dozens of agents and companies which provide you with the ability to see what rental units are available. Use these search results to see what you can get for your money.

Once you've found the short list of rental units:

1. **Figure out what it is really going to cost.** Rent is not the only factor to consider. Utilities (trash, water, heat), rental insurance, and miscellaneous commuting costs (fuel, vehicle wear and tear, tolls, etc.) are costs that you need to consider when establishing what you will actually pay. Expect to also pay at least the first and last month's rent plus a security deposit.

2. **Do not rush.** Fully evaluate and inspect every unit and write down your important questions before walking through the units. Never sign anything prior to seeing the unit personally. Take all of the paperwork to JAG before you sign. JAG Soldiers are responsible for protecting you from entering into disadvantageous legal arrangements and they will assist you with contracts, agreements, etc. Utilize them. Once a lease is signed, you've entered into a legally binding contract.

3. **Get a receipt** for all payment between you and the landlord. Itemize the receipt to show security deposit, first and last month's rent, utilities (if they are included), etc.

Buying

The process for buying begins similarly to renting. Contact your post's housing office, get information, and conduct research on property value and cost, while evaluating potential properties in person.

House Hunting Tips:

What is your intent with this house?

- To rent after you PCS?
- To retire in?
- To sell and hopefully make a profit?
- To provide a secure location for your family to live?
- Understand that realtors get paid a percentage of the purchase price of your home. It is in **their** interest to sell you the most expensive house you can afford.
- Location is critical. Narrow your search to the right location. The perfect house in a bad location is NOT the perfect house.

- Do your homework and make a list of the homes you find during your research.
- Take notes and pictures of each house. After seeing ten houses you will start to forget what you liked or didn't like about each one
- Take your time. If you have to go beyond the 10 day Permissive TDY window, then do so. Do not rush the biggest purchase of your life.

The differences between buying and renting become clear as you seek to pay for your new home. Very few Soldiers have more than $100,000 in cash, so chances are that you are going to finance (take out a loan) the purchase of your new home.

Loans and Other House Purchase Costs

1. **VA loan**—As a member of the Army you can use the VA loan (**www.benefits.va.gov/homeloans**). If you are on active duty and have served for 181 days, you are eligible. Use this loan on your residence (not rental property) and you can avoid Primary Mortgage Insurance, which is an insurance payable by you but which protects (and is required by the issuer of your loan) to protect the bank if you default on your loan. You can apply for other loans like FHA, but explore what your VA mortgage benefits package can offer.

Types of Common Home Loans

30-year fixed: Fixed monthly payments over 30 years, low monthly payments, but lots of interest paid in the long-term.

15-year fixed: Fixed monthly payments; pay over 15 years, which means higher monthly payments than 30-year, but less interest in long-term.

Balloon: Structured similar to 30-year fixed, but after five to seven years the remaining balance must be paid either out-of-pocket or through refinance. Risky, but low, fixed monthly payments through a five to seven year period.

Adjustable Rate Mortgages (ARMs): Interest rate adjusts every month with no adjustment cap. Low payment initially, but can rise steeply.

Bimonthly: Slight interest advantage by having two payments per month. On the average 30-year mortgage this will shorten mortgage by one month.

2. **Down payment.** Your down payment will generally be between 3 and 20%, depending on the loan type.
3. **Random costs.** Get an estimate of closing costs, taxes, county and state fees, inspections, and insurance from your agent or attorney.
4. **Property taxes.** Many lenders will require you to set aside money for the payment of property taxes, in an escrow account. Sometimes this will be added to your mortgage and you will pay a percentage of your annual taxes each month. The average annual tax rate is about 1.5% of your purchase price.
5. **Maintenance.** HouseMaster, a home inspection company with 300 franchises nationwide, published typical costs of some major home repairs:

- Roofing: $1500–$5000
- Electrical: $200–$1500
- Plumbing: $300–$5000
- Central air: $800–$2500
- Central heating: $1500–$3000
- Structure: $1500–$3000

Benefits of Home Ownership

- **Capital gains exclusion**—live in your home for two years out of the last five years (and there are some special accommodations made for Soldiers) and you do not have to pay capital gains taxes at the time of sale on profits up to $250, 000 per individual and $500,000 per married couple.
- **Appreciation**—historically around 5% annual appreciation in home price, although recent changes in the housing market have shaken this statistic.
- **Tax deductions—Some or all of mortgage interest is deductible** (IRS Publication 530, Tax Information for Homeowner).
- **Equity**—the difference between what your home is worth and what you owe on the mortgage. This value can be used to apply for additional low interest loans against the equity in the home.
- **Selling**—if you sell your house for less than you bought it you can write off the amount lost as a deduction when you file your taxes.

Use a home mortgage calculator and track your mortgage payment details (www.mortgagecalculator.org/).

Final Note

Decide where to live based on the needs of your family and the realities of your finances. The site *www.ahrn.com* is a great government website that provides information and advice for housing.

There is nothing more admirable than when two people who see eye to eye keep house as man and wife.

Homer
Greek Epic Poet

Marriage

BLUF:
There are dozens of books that are written about the complexities of marriage, specifically within the Army. This chapter provides an overview of some of the major financial benefits of marriage, and the primary Army resources that help you and your family.

Discussion:
Make sure that you (the Soldier) and your spouse are aware of all the benefits for which you are eligible.
• How to "add a spouse" to the Army system
• Financial benefits to marriage

Dependents 101
An Army spouse is entitled to a large number of on-post services, but before he or she can begin taking advantage of these opportunities and services you must add them to the "Army system."

How to accomplish this:
1. **Secure an original copy of your marriage certificate.** The exact document varies from state to state, but the key words are "official marriage license."
2. **Enroll in the Defense Enrollment Reporting System (DEERS).** This allows dependents to receive medical benefits. *Be prepared to present a marriage license, birth certificates, and social security cards for each dependent you are enrolling.* Your duty station should have a DEERs desk or office at the same location that you initially in-process.
3. **Obtain a military I.D. card for your spouse.** In order to gain access to the PX, commissary, gym, library and other military benefits your spouse will need an ID card. In fact, all dependents over the age of 10 must have an ID card in order to use post services. Your post's ID card issuing facility will provide you with the specific instructions, but be prepared to show a copy of your marriage license, birth certificate, and a photo ID.

The best and most comprehensive resource to determine benefits and services that you and your family are entitled to is Military One Source.

4. **Get additional pay.** Make sure that your pay reflects that you have a dependent. A dependent provides you with an increase in BAH (or establishes a justification for receiving BAH if you are ranked below E-6 and are not already receiving BAH). Your S-1 is the primary resource for this inclusion.

5. **Register your spouse's vehicle.** These decals are usually given out at the main MP station. *Be prepared to show current registration and insurance, driver's license and your military ID.*

6. **Update insurance beneficiary.** Update all insurance policies. Your S-1 will direct you to the proper on-post service charged with updating this.

7. **Legal.** Get free counsel from a JAG officer on the benefits of a power of attorney, filing joint taxes, and other legal implications of marriage. Information on free JAG legal assistance can be found at legal assistance. **http://www.legalassistance.law.af.mil**

Family Resources

The best and most comprehensive resource to determine benefits and services that you and your family are entitled to is Military One Source located at **www.militaryonesource.mil.**

Final Note

Financially, marriage entitles you to BAH (or a BAH increase), which can be a significant increase in many cases. Conversely, marriage also often incurs a number of substantial expenses. This section is short because the decision to get married SHOULD NEVER be a financial one. That said however, finances should be taken into consideration with each decision that you make

The secret of financial success is to spend what you have left after saving, instead of saving what is left after spending.

Unknown

Where to Get Financial Help

BLUF:

As we have suggested throughout this guide, an excellent way to learn more about the policies and products that you already own is to pick up the phone and contact those companies that you may already be using and ask them to explain the investment, insurance coverage, etc. that you already hold with them.

Discussion:

This chapter serves as a reference and a reminder that sometimes the best help comes at a financial cost. Often it is better to research and pay for financial help, rather than taking matters into your own hands to make ill-informed financial decisions that can affect your financial future. Fortunately for Soldiers, there is a host of FREE financial support available, from Army contracted financial planners and legal advisors, to excellent financial institutions and foundations.

Financial Advisor

If you decide to seek out a financial advisor, do your homework first. "Financial advisor" is a very broad term that is often used to describe stockbrokers, insurance sales people, and mortgage brokers, as well as generalist financial planners. Know what service you're looking for and then seek out professionals with expertise in that field. Some advisors deal in a specific area such as life insurance or mutual fund sales. Others, generally called financial planners, provide a broader range of advice in areas such as retirement planning, overall insurance planning, cash flow analysis, investment planning, and estate planning.

Fortunately for Army Soldiers, there is a host of free financial support available, from Army-contracted financial planners and legal advisors, to excellent financial institutions and foundations.

One of the most important questions you want to ask a potential financial advisor is, "How are you and your company being paid for the advice you are giving me?" This will help you determine where your financial advisors' interests are. Listed below are three common ways that financial advisors are paid:

1. **Commission**—the advisor gets paid at the time of a transaction, such as a purchase of insurance or the purchase or sale of a stock or mutual fund;

2. **Fee-Based**—the advisor gets paid through some combination of fees for a service that is provided to you and commissions on transactions —the purchase and/or sale of products;

3. **Fee-Only**—the advisor's compensation consists solely of fees paid directly by you to the advisor or the advisor's company for the service that is provided to you. This kind of advisor does not receive commissions for transactions.

Key credentials to look for when selecting your financial planner:

a. **CFP**—Certified Financial Planner
b. **CHFC**—Chartered Financial Consultant
c. **PFS**—Personal Finance Specialist

Legal Support

Your local JAG office provides sound legal advice and many times legal and financial advice are related. Before you enter any financially binding contract, such as a rental lease, make sure that contract is reviewed, because signing on the dotted line can have harsh repercussions on your personal finances. Reference your base directory to set up an office call with your local JAG office: this advice is free and easily accessible.

Self-Help

The Internet has a limitless amount of resources to help you plan, research and succeed as you hurdle the financial obstacles encountered throughout your life. However, keep in mind that with abundant online resources also comes fraudulent websites, predatory lending organizations and biased opinions. To help you find your way clear, here are initial screening tools you can use to avoid some pitfalls:

a. Viable financial institutions such as Vanguard, USAA, and the Bank of America are organizations that put a high value on their brand. Their information tends to be less subjective and more factual to mitigate chances of misinterpretation or lawsuits. Warning: Specified accounts, such as "Vanguard 500 Index Fund" are going to be solicited on Vanguard and not by USAA.

b. Reading a prospectus or a company's balance charts is not easily interpreted, but can provide a wealth of information. This information is supposed to represent a company's financial health.

c. Scholarly sources are often great pieces of information where much of the work and research has been done for you. Publications such as CNN Money and Investopedia.com are good websites to facilitate research.

d. Calculators are provided on many websites of viable financial institutions that allow the personal investors to manipulate numbers for their personal situation. This helps you, the investor, to understand what your ideal interest rate is, how much you have to save each year for your son's college, or how much you should have in retirement. USAA.com; Mint.com; BankofAmerica.com all provide multiple different calculators.

e. Know what the finance words mean! As you build your financial education you will quickly realize that the finance world operates with a different lingo. Understand the terms and you will better understand what's happening with your money. One of the best resources for easy-to-understand definitions is Investopedia.com.

Final Note

There are experts that can "fill the gaps" in your financial knowledge. Don't hesitate to pick up the phone or email around and talk to several of these experts in order to have a better understanding of what you can do with your money.

Parting Guidance

Financial Responsibility is a Choice

A career in the Army provides the opportunity to accumulate wealth, but inevitably, career Soldiers often find themselves falling short of their financial goals. This Soldier's Financial Leadership Guide will help answer the questions that you always had about Army finance, and will provide you with a path to guide you along a life of financial responsibility and independence.

The Soldier's Financial Leadership Guide will provide you with the understanding, resources, references and means to gaining financial responsibility. It is designed to serve as a "one stop shop" for Army financial questions, and will prove to be a guide that every Soldier chooses to keep within "arms reach." This quick reference guide will answer the questions you have always wanted to ask: when and why an Army Do It Yourself Move (DITY) is recommended; the benefits of an Army Thrift Savings Plan (TSP); how to pay for college/further education for you or your spouse while you are still on active duty; how to repair and build credit; how and when to finance a house and countless other important financial life decisions.

This guide attempts to convey a lot in a little. It uses graphs, statistics, and short anecdotes in order to explain important concepts in simple terms. Each chapter is formatted Army-style with the bottom line up front, and followed by background information and short anecdotes. This book was written to provide clear, concise financial information for Army members and dependants.

LDR Investments, LLP ("LDR")—Legal Disclaimer

This publication is not designed to provide personal financial planning advice or consultation. It is in no way affiliated with the United States Government or any of its entities, any financial and/or investment firm(s). The role of LDR Investments, LLP is to provide financial communication advice not investment advice.

No warranties

This publication is provided "as is" without any representations or warranties, express or implied. LDR makes no representations or warranties in relation to this publication or the information and materials provided in this publication. Without prejudice to the generality of the foregoing paragraph, LDR does not warrant that:
• This publication will be constantly available, or available at all; or
• The information in this publication is complete, true, accurate or
  non-misleading.
Nothing in this publication constitutes, or is meant to constitute, advice of any kind. [If you require advice in relation to any [legal, financial or medical] matter you should consult an appropriate professional.]

Limitations of liability

LDR will not be liable to you (whether under the law of contact, the law of torts or otherwise) in relation to the contents of, or use of, or otherwise in connection with, this publication:
• for any indirect, special or consequential loss; or
• for any business losses, loss of revenue, income, profits or anticipated savings, loss of contracts or business relationships, loss of reputation or goodwill, or loss or corruption of information or data.
These limitations of liability apply even if LDR has been expressly advised of the potential loss.

Exceptions

Nothing in this publication disclaimer will exclude or limit any warranty implied by law that it would be unlawful to exclude or limit; and nothing in this publication disclaimer will exclude or limit LDR's liability in respect of any:
• death or personal injury caused by LDR's negligence;
• fraud or fraudulent misrepresentation on the part of LDR or
• matter which it would be illegal or unlawful for LDR to exclude or limit, or to attempt or purport to exclude or limit, its liability.

Reasonableness

By using this publication, you agree that the exclusions and limitations of liability set out in this publication disclaimer are reasonable. If you do not think they are reasonable, you must not use this publication.

Other parties

You accept that, as a limited liability entity, LDR has an interest in limiting the personal liability of its officers and employees. You agree that you will not bring any claim personally against LDR officers or employees in respect of any losses you suffer in connection with the publication. Without prejudice to the foregoing paragraph, you agree that the limitations of warranties and liability set out in this publication disclaimer will protect LDR officers, employees, agents, subsidiaries, successors, assigns and sub-contractors as well as LDR officers in their respective individual capacities.

Unenforceable provisions

If any provision of this publication disclaimer is, or is found to be, unenforceable under applicable law, that will not affect the enforceability of the other provisions of this publication disclaimer.

Author Biographies

Richard Sexton

Rich graduated from Mercer University ROTC as the number one member of his commissioning class, and then commissioned as an Infantry Officer. After earning Ranger, Airborne and Air Assault qualifications, Rich deployed in support of OIF, where he served as a Rifle Platoon Leader and as a Company Executive Officer. For actions during this deployment, Rich was awarded the Col. Scooter Burke Award, given to the officer that shows the most leadership potential in the Battalion. Rich excelled in Army combatives, becoming a 1st Infantry

Division Champion and earning a spot on the Ft. Riley Combatives Team. This gave him the opportunity to be the team's captain, and led the team to a second place finish at the All-Army Combatives Tournament in 2009 and 2010. Currently Rich is assigned to Special Operations Command South in Florida.

Lauren Gore

Lauren graduated from the United States Military Academy in 2007 and commissioned as an Infantry Officer. After joining the 4th Brigade Combat Team, 1st Infantry Division he served as a Mortar Platoon Leader, a Light Infantry Company Executive Officer deployed to OIF, and as the assistant Battalion Operations Officer. In between these assignments Lauren twice represented the 1st Infantry Division at the U.S. Army Best Ranger Competition. Most recently CPT Gore was assigned to the United States Military Academy at West Point. Lauren is a member of Harvard Law School, class of 2015.

JD Dolan

JD graduated with honors from Dickinson College in 2007 where he was designated a Distinguished Military Graduate. He was awarded a four-year Army ROTC Scholarship, with the goal of ultimately serving as an Infantry Officer. While in college, he graduated from the US Army Airborne School and was the Distinguished Honor Graduate of his Regiment at the Officer Basic Leader Course at Ft. Lewis, WA and later attended US Army Ranger School, where he was the Distinguished Honor Graduate of his class and received the General William O. Darby Award. After a deployment to Iraq as a Rifle Platoon Leader with the 10th Mountain Division, JD joined the

1st Battalion, 75th Ranger Regiment. He has had three deployments to Afghanistan with the Rangers, the last two as a Rifle Platoon Leader and Strike Force Commander.

CPSIA information can be obtained at www.ICGtesting.com
Printed in the USA
LVOW010828220812

295400LV00002B/1/P

9 780985 406103